# Pygmy Goats
# Miniature Goats and Pygmy
# A Guide to Keeping Pyg

## By

## George Hoddington

# Table of Contents

# Introduction

Pygmy goats are great animals to keep, either as pets, companion animals or as an alternative dairy option. They are both entertaining and very useful. They do fantastic work keeping the lawn cropped and keeping other animals company. They produce good quality milk without having to be mated every year.

A Pygmy goat is also a fantastic addition to an existing herd, being strong and of good temperament and having a calming influence on their peers and herd mates. They also make a good basis to cross from and have a good, wide gene pool.

The decision to keep any animal is a big one and you need to be informed. You need to know about any special housing requirements. You need to know what they eat and if they call for any dietary additions. You need to know about any potential breeding complications. You need to know the benefits of owning them too, and make sure that there are many pros and it's not just a massive list of cons.

What you need at this stage of the game is information. This book will tell you all you need to know in order to make the rest of this decision. If you are seriously considering having goats as pets, then you must prepare yourself for a great deal of responsibility that is about to come your way.

However, the most important thing that you need to understand when you are bringing home a pet goat is that this animal needs special care and attention. Yes, the regular pets like cats and dogs need the same amount of care. However, the advantage that you have with these conventional pets is that you have enough support and also a lot of information available about the health and care of these animals.

As for goats, they are seldom found in the urban set up. They are usually raised in large numbers on farms and also in designated commercial set ups where there is ample professional help available to take care of these animals. If you are planning to bring a goat home, on the other hand, you must invest a lot more time doing your homework and research about this animal in the first place. You must be sure that you can take on this responsibility before you make a commitment.

You see, the goat is a large animal. This means that you need to have enough space in your home to begin with. It is definitely not possible, and even unethical to cram a goat up in a tiny apartment. They need exercise and a lot of space in order to remain healthy.

You may choose to keep your goat in your backyard or even in a designated space outdoors. Once you do that, you need to worry about keeping them fenced and protected. If you are keeping a goat in an urban set up, the last thing you want is your pet goat breaking free and running out into the freeway.

When you bring a goat home, you must be prepared to let it stay true to its instincts. If you find a goat cute, that's alright. However, if you expect your goat to cuddle up and sleep in the same bed with you, it is time for you to consider other options for a pet. Your goat will not fetch the morning newspaper or sit on the couch while you watch TV either! It is an "outdoor" pet. This is a very important thing you need to tell yourself several times before you bring home a goat.

Now, if you are willing to let the goat be a goat, you need to progress on to the next step. The kind of food and the care that your goat needs is pretty different from the conventional pet. They have specific requirements that help them stay healthy. We will discuss that in more detail. However, what you must understand is that clean drinking water and the right kind of food is extremely essential for your goat's health.

Does a goat need more attention than other pets? Yes! These animals depict certain behavioural patterns that may require a good deal of attention, at least in the beginning. For instance, a goat needs to relieve itself a lot more than other pets. While training the goat could be possible, the time you need to spend is a lot more than a cat or a dog.

Although it may seem like having a goat is nothing but trouble, let me tell you that if you are really a "goat type" of person, this animal can be extremely rewarding! You can find a great companion in a goat! They are extremely docile creatures and are quite entertaining when they are in a herd. They will interact with you, head butt you when you don't pay attention and even follow you around if they are fond of you. The kids are extremely adorable. Watching them progress from simply stumbling to prancing around your yard is the best thing you can experience.
As for the commercial side to having goats, you can benefit a lot from breeding goats if you know how to do it right. If you have a rare breed that you want to breed and multiply in numbers, you can learn the art or seek assistance from professionals.

The next thing is showing your goats. There are several pet shows that have a special category for farm animals like goats. If you are interested in exhibiting your pet, you will have a lot to do from the word GO. You need to groom and take very good care of your goat.

Of course, on a larger scale, goat's milk is a good business venture. However that requires a good deal of investment. In any case, you can have access to fresh goat milk for your entire family, for sure!
Of course, not everyone needs to be an "expert" at goat keeping. But, you need to be prepared with all the information that you need. This book covers all the subjects including how to choose a suitable breed, how to take care of the goat, how to feed them and even how to ensure that they are always healthy. If you are a first time goat owner, this is the perfect book for you.

# Chapter 1. Miniature Goats and Pygmy Goats as Pets

The latest revolution among goat owners across the globe is keeping miniature goats and pygmy goats as pets. Some even believe that the pygmy goat might as well be the new replacement for common house pets like the dog!

The best thing about pygmy goats is that they make great urban pets. They are perfectly sized to be housed in the limitations that are present in the city. On the other hand, they are productive like the regular goat breeds that provide milk and beautiful fabric like cashmere.

Pygmy goats are becoming so popular these days that they are redefining urban farming. In many countries, it is possible to acquire a license for these goats just as you would get a license for a cat or a dog.
Although the goat is a farm animal, the prospects of having them in an urban set up has made room for several bills and rules about having them at home. With the advent of pygmy goats, people are opting for an alternate kind of pet in their homes.

The reason for the popularity of the pygmy goats is their ability to produce milk. Many people are allergic to cow or buffalo milk. Having a goat at home gives them the opportunity to prepare cheese and also benefit from the high quality milk that is produced by these breeds.

While pygmy goat ownership is allowed in cities like Denver and Seattle, there are other cities like Michigan where the decision of keeping goats can be approved or denied by the community that plans to keep goats as pets. So it means that you will have to consult with your neighbours and your local authorities before you bring home a pygmy goat.

Either way, the rules regarding the pygmy goats are meant to help goat owners understand the seriousness of keeping goats at home. So when you bring home a pygmy goat, you must be aware of the responsibilities associated with it.

There are two types of pygmy goats that you can bring home. The original small sized goats that originated from some genetic mutation in the regular goats. The other type is the pygmy version of the regular barn goats that are the result of mixed breeding.

# Identifying a pygmy goat

You can identify a pygmy goat by the size of an adult goat. The size of a pygmy goat is perhaps, the most alluring quality for an urban goat lover. They are smaller, which means that they need less space. Also, the investment necessary in the shelters is smaller in comparison to the regular goat breeds.

Since the size of the pygmy goat matters, it is important to know how large they can actually get. So, to make it easier to perceive, let us compare a Nigerian Dwarf Goat to the average barn goat.

The height of goats is usually measured at the withers. This is the measurement from the hoof till the point at which the shoulder blade stops. A regular, adult barn goat will grow to a height of 30 inches at the withers. Most pygmy goats will grow to about 16 or 20 inches. That makes them almost half the size of a regular barn dairy goat.

If it is still hard for you to picture, let me give you another comparison. A fully grown medium sized dog, like the Labrador is about 25 inches at the withers. On an average, an adult pygmy goat is about 16 inches. However, the maximum height of a pygmy goat can go up to 22 inches.

This means that a Nigerian Dwarf Goat can be almost as large as a fully grown Labrador. So, if you are bringing home pygmy goat kids, you must plan all your preparations for a goat that can get that big.

# Chapter 2. Why Choose Miniature Goats as Pets?

Now that you have decided to bring home goats and keep them as pets, you need to be clear about the reason why you are keeping goats in the first place. There are a few advantages of knowing the purpose of goat keeping well in advance. They are:

·You will know what breed to pick

·You will be able to prepare better for the breed that you are bringing home

·You will also know exactly what to expect from your goat in terms of financial gains. You will also be able to work out your finances accordingly.

·You can be better prepared for the common health hazards with these goat breeds.

The benefits of raising a herd of goats are many. However, before you get into the benefits, let me tell you about the basic reasons why people keep goats as pets:

## Raising goats for dairy

The milk provided by goats is considered to be extremely nutritious. Goat cheese is often a very lucrative business for most people who bring home goats for milking. There are certain breeds that are extremely popular if you are interested in a lucrative milking business. The recommended breeds are La Manca, Pygmy Goat, Alpine Goat, Oberhasli, Sable and Mini Goats.

## Raising goats for meat

For those who are looking for a pet goat, the idea of raising a goat for meat may seem downright cruel. However, it is a fact that raising goats for meat has proved to be one of the most lucrative business options for several goat owners across the globe. When you are raising goats for meat, the obvious requirements are a decent size of the breed and a certain quality of meat that the goat must be able to provide. The most recommended breeds for meat are the Tennessee Goats, the Spanish Goats and the Kiko goats.

### Meat production

If you are raising a herd for meat production, you may obtain the meat either by sending the selected herd to the slaughter house directly or through livestock markets.

In the livestock markets, you may exchange the herd for another breed or a younger herd or for cash. From there, they are sent to the production unit. Whether you are going directly or through a market or not, your herd requires an FCI or a Food Chain Information. This is a legal requirement that lists the health details of your herd. The objective of the FCI is to ensure the quality and the safety of the meat that you are providing. You can obtain an FCI declaration from websites of food standard agencies in your country or from abattoirs. Even your local agriculture department will be able to help you with this.

### Reduce amount of grains in the feed
If you want your doe to stop producing milk then you have to reduce the amount of grains it eats. This will reduce its energy intake and this will adversely affect milk production. This is very essential in helping the doe to reduce its production of milk because it will help it gain more weight. There are other options that will help you supplement on the doe diet such as fodder and silage. You need to keep it in a shed because you will have to closely monitor what it is eating all the time.

### Advantages of "drying up" a doe
There are several advantages. One of them is that it helps the doe be able to gain weight and look healthier if it has started looking wasted. The second is that it helps the kid to be able to learn to feed on grain and fodder. It also prepares the doe for the next delivery by storing up essential nutrients. One needs to be able to check for mastitis and other illnesses as they occur a lot during this period of drying up. Drying up a doe may take time and one should not hurry up the process. Eventually this does happen even naturally without any help.

## What Is The Proper Age To "Band" A Male Kid Goat?
Just like the size of a human family, the rate of reproduction of domestic animals needs to be controlled. Banding is the process of castrating and removing testicles by using a rubber band. However, this process has to be done at the correct time. So, what is the proper age To "Band" a male kid goat?

The age to band a male goat depends on:
1. Management style preferred by the producer.
2. Market demands.
3. Culture.

However, most producers prefer to band kid goats within three months of birth. The reason being that male kid goats tend to reach sexual maturity at a very young age. Consequently, it can impregnate any she-goat without your knowledge.

An Animal Health Survey completed in 2008 showed that 77% of all male goats are castrated. The average banding age among the producers was found to be 22.3 days. This low banding age was attributed to the better feed, which ensure that sexual maturity is reached early. The study advised that if a producer preferred banding after 3 months, the male kid goat needs to be separated from the females.

### *Benefits of Early Kid Castration*
Obviously, it ensures that unwanted pregnancies do not occur. This way, the young kid-goats do not have an opportunity to impregnate their sisters (interbreeding) leading to weak genes being transmitted. Only the male with the preferred characteristics should be allowed to mate with a selected female.

As much as the young he-goat may be sexually mature, the young she-goats it mates (sisters or not) may not be ready. The probability of the goat dying during birth is increased by 13.6% if this happens. A kid goat born from an immature mother often has deformities.
Testosterone is a hormone that gives mammals their male sexual characteristics. In addition, this hormone produced by the testicles is associated with troublesomeness. Subsequently, a castrated male goat is easier to handle. It also grows faster because no energy is directed to sexuality.

### *How banding works*
As the word suggests, a rubber band referred to as an elastrator is used. This band is put on the neck of the scrotum, taking care not to band over the rudimentary teats. Since no nutrients or blood enters the scrotum, its mass atrophies and detaches with time. After it falls off, the area is disinfected with iodine.

### *Advantages of Banding over Other Methods of Castration*
Firstly, this is the most popular method of castration. In fact, the Animal Health Survey mentioned above stated that 90% of farmers preferred this method. Their reasons were:
- This procedure is relatively easy and can be done without any expertise

- Since it is the most preferred method, economies of scale dictate that it is cheap.
- Does not involve shedding of blood.
- It is generally considered more humane than other methods.
- The risk of infections after the procedure is done is relatively low.
- To relieve pain, especially in the first hour, anesthesia can be used.

Now that the question: 'What Is the Proper Age to "Band" male Kid Goats?' has been answered, it is wise to ensure hygiene while doing it. In addition, the band manufacturer's instructions need to be followed. For further information, consult an expert.

## How to raise a Pygmy Goat

The actual practice associated with raising goats nowadays appears to be quite popular. Many individuals are trying their own hand along with raising these types of animals either like a commercial venture or just as a means of introducing a brand new pet to the family. Obviously, there is really a huge distinction between increasing goats with regard to profit as well as giving implementing a pet for the home. Nevertheless, this article will attempt to cover a few of the basic essentials to begin on course successfully.

### How you can raise goats suggestion #1:

Try to find the breed associated with goats that will meet your requirements. Farming goats might mean with regard to meat, with regard to fiber or even for whole milk. It may also mean you want to adopt a number of as domestic pets. If you're choosing the former, attempt to choose goats which are suitable with regard to meat or even wool or even milk manufacturing. If you're choosing the latter, try to find the more docile breeds such as the Miniature, Anglo-Pygmy or even South Africa Boer goats.

### How you can raise goats suggestion #2:

One thing you need to remember regarding goats is these are herd creatures, which means that they're happiest once they share areas with additional goats, as well as other plantation or house animals. You might like to introduce your pet goat to existing pets at an extremely young age (occasionally they relationship well using the horses or even dogs); in order to make the transition comfortable for both.

### *How you can raise goats suggestion #3:*
Goats are extremely active creatures. They would rather cover lengthy distances whenever grazing and they may be especially fun and lively throughout the day. Apart from providing all of them ample grazing places, you may also want to supply them non-toxic playthings like golf balls, boulders or even tires. A goat that isn't mentally triggered or one which is cooped up inside a small living area can turn out to be destructive and much more prone to hurt itself or others around it.

### *How to raise goats suggestion #4:*
Supply your creatures with proper real estate with individual beddings as well as feeding or watering channels. Keeping them inside a barn as well as throwing all of them feeds each and every few hours only will not do whatsoever. This might make your goats vulnerable to diseases along with other illnesses. Keep their own bedding areas free of anything the goats shouldn't be eating (which includes their own droppings) and permit them sufficient space to maneuver within. As a rule, one goat would want about four meters of living area.

## How Expensive Are Pygmy Goats To Keep?
Just as the name suggests, Pygmy goats are small in size compared to any other breed of goat. Their small size does not limit the amount of milk that they can produce. They can be reared to provide milk as well as meat. However, a large number of people prefer to rear them as a pet due to their cute appearance. Due to their small size Pygmy goats are economical to rear, as they don't feed much compared to other breeds. Nevertheless, there are essential things that you should do to ensure that you keep Pygmy goats healthy.

On average a Pygmy goat can cost about 150-300 dollars.
First you have to ensure that you give the goat healthy feeds. The feeds must be rich in Vitamins D and A. These can be obtained from green hay and green grass as well as yellow corn. In addition, Vitamin D can be acquired naturally from the sunlight. Therefore one thing to invest in when planning to rear Pygmy goats is the feed. You can buy feeds in advance before you bring the goat home to ensure that it won't lack food. The feeding can be done throughout the day but it should not be done less than two times a day.

The second thing to invest in when planning to raise a Pygmy goat is shelter. Pygmy goats must be sheltered in a clean environment that is well ventilated. This breed of goat is not hardy like others and therefore it cannot survive in poor conditions. It is prone to illness if proper care lacks and it can even die. The shelter should provide a nice sleeping place such as an area filled with sawdust or dry soft grass. The shelter should also be secure from wild animals such as dogs and other predators. First ensure that you have a good shelter in place before you buy a Pygmy goat.

Another cost that is incurred in rearing Pygmy goats is in health care. This breed requires good health care since it is not hardy like other breeds. It requires regular vaccination and de-worming for it to stay in a healthy condition. It can easily contract diseases if proper care is not taken; also this breed is prone to bone diseases. Other health measures that should be taken when rearing this breed include trimming the hooves as well as brushing the coat.

Last but not the least; invest in providing the goats with clean fresh water. Water is very essential when rearing goats, lack of water can cause illness in goats. The best way to provide clean fresh water is to construct a small tank where the goats can drink fresh water. The water should be running to ensure that it's always fresh.

In conclusion, the cost of raising a Pygmy goat is great but there are basic things that must be put into consideration to ensure that the goat stays in good health. Shelter, feeds and fresh water are the main basic things to invest in when rearing a Pygmy goat.

## What Type Of Housing Do Pygmy Goats Need?

A lot of information is available about dairy goats and their housing. But what type of housing do pygmy goats need? People find it really difficult to answer this question because there is not enough information available for common knowledge. All types of goats should be kept stress free and enough attention should be given to protect them from snow, wind and rain. The pygmy goats are not different at all. They also need all these facilities like other types of goats. There are different interpretations regarding various methods to be used for the housing of these types of goats. Some people have been using basic types of sheds while some others advocate the importance of more elaborate kinds of housing to the pygmy goats.

What type of housing do pygmy goats need? A convincing answer to this question depends on a number of factors. The budget plays an important role and you should also be able to clean the shed with great amount of ease and comfort. The barn for the pygmy goats should be comfortable for both the goats and the owner. Enough space should be there for the pygmy goats to move around and on an average 15 to 20 square feet per animal should be allocated to promote healthy living space. Enough care should be taken to keep it draft free as well. Benches can be installed in these barns so that the pygmy goats can relax and enjoy them during mild weather conditions. They do not like to sleep on the ground and that is why the benches will come in very handy. During hostile weather conditions they will cuddle under the benches and rubber mats covered with sawdust and straw can be used as bedding in these weather conditions. Built-in hay mangers should be installed to keep the hay well below the ground level because the pygmy goats will not eat the hay that falls on the ground.

One of the best ways to answer the question, 'what type of housing do pygmy goats need', is to advise the usage of wood as the material for the construction. The flooring can be made with wood, concrete or clay depending on the climatic conditions and the budget. The smell of the urine will get stuck in the wood and it will rot out after some time. The dampness of concrete surface can create problems for the pygmy goats and veterinarians advocate the importance of a surface with a thick layer of clay on top of a gravel base. All the disadvantages associated with other types of surfaces can be averted with it and the clay can be re-laid after two to three years to keep it fresh.

Good fencing is absolutely essential to keep the pygmy goats safe from predators. The barn or housing should have a trough or buckets for water and this water should be changed every day to keep it clean and safe. Proper ventilation is absolutely essential to provide a healthy environment for Pygmy goats. A good structure of the housing for pygmy goats should look like a properly ventilated three sided shed or a large sized doghouse, like the Igloo-type.

# Chapter 3. The Best Miniature Goat, Pygmy Goat Breeds

There are several breeds of mini goats that have swept the urban farming market. Breeders are experimenting with several existing breeds to create newer pygmy breeds. The type of breed that you are looking for depends on the purpose that you have in mind for the goat. There are a couple of breeds that are considered the best for goat owners. You can choose a breed that suits your requirements and also your personality.

## 1. Nigerian Dwarf Goat

The Nigerian Dwarf Goat is easily the most popular breed among the pygmy goats. It is the descendant of a Central African Goat breed. The Nigerian Dwarf goat resembles a regular alpine dairy goat. It is smaller in size and is known for its proportionate body, unlike its cousin, the pygmy goat. The Nigerian Dwarf breed became one of the most popular pygmy breeds because of the variety of coat colors available. While the base colors were mostly brown, black and gold, several mixed coat colors have evolved as a result of breeding.

*History of the breed:*
The Nigerian Dwarf breed originated from a Central African breed. A genetic defect called pituitary hypoplasia led to dwarfism in the Central African Breed. Owing to the quality of milk produced by this breed, it soon flourished in the region. Thereafter, it was shipped to the United States to feed big cats in the zoo. As breeders realised the value of this breed in an urban set up, it was recognised as a separate breed by the American Goat Association and was exported all over the world.

*Pros of the breed:*
- Intelligent, friendly and docile breed
- Small size that is easy to manage.
- They come in a variety of colors and may also have blue eyes.
- They breed all year around
- Perfect size for children and even people who have disabilities.
- Known for therapeutic qualities
- Kidding is very easy
- They usually have twins

*Cons of the breed:*
- They are able to produce only one quart of milk each day. This is not good enough if you are looking at a serious milking business.
- This breed is still considered a novelty which makes showing a little difficult.
- They may have small udders like sheep, sometimes.

## 2. Pygmy Goat

For a long time, all the pygmy goats were called pygmy goats. However, these goats have a distinct body structure that makes them very easy to identify. Pygmy goats are known for their short legs. They have a very large body cavity that makes them appear stocky and heavy. These goats have a round belly that is their most distinct feature. Pygmy goats are usually seen in solid black, brown and white shades. They also have certain distinct markings that are considered favourable. The agouti coloration is also common among the pygmy goat. The pygmy goat also makes the perfect companion for those who are interested in having entertaining pets. They are extremely playful and fun to be around.

*History of the Pygmy Goat:*
The history of the pygmy breed is quite similar to the history of the
Nigerian Dwarf breed. Both breeds are descendants of the Central African
breeds. The type of dwarfism is what sets them apart. The pygmy goat was
the result of a type of dwarfism called achondroplasia. This breed was also
brought to the USA to feed big cats and became a popular breed
eventually. The pygmy goat produces great quality milk and is also very
easy to maintain. Since they are smaller, they are also safe to have around
children. As a result, pygmy goats became a popular breed across the USA
and eventually across the world.

*Pros of the breed:*
·      Very entertaining and playful
·      Extremely intelligent and friendly.
·      Perfect for children
·      They are easy to house in the urban setting.
·      The quality of milk produced is extremely high
·      They are highly therapeutic.
·      They breed all year around.

*Cons of the breed:*
·      Kids tend to get lost very easily.
·      They will eat just about anything, including sand, which leads to
intestinal problems.
·      Susceptible to several health disorders.

# 3. Kinder Goat

Today there are thousands of Kinder goats that have been registered. As a
result, this is recognised as a unique breed and there is also a special
Kinder Goat Breeders association. The kinder goat can grow to be close to
26 inches in height. For this reason, these goats are considered medium
sized goats by several goat enthusiasts. However, most often, they retain
the size deemed correct for a goat categorised as a miniature. This goat is
accepted in any color and with any type of coat marking.

*History of the breed:*
The first specimen of the kinder goat was created in the year 1985. During
the breeding season, a Pygmy Buck died on the Zederkamm Farm. As a
result, two does that were on the farm did not have any mate. The owners
of the Zederkamm farm did not want to take their does to any other farm.
So, they decided to mate the Pygmy does with the pygmy goats that were
already present on the farm. The breeders wanted to get the height of the
goats right. Finally, in the year 1985, the first set of Kinders was born.

There were three in the set. By 2009, three thousand Kinders had been registered. The breed became popular for several unique qualities and was shipped across the globe.

*Pros of the breed:*
- The breed is extremely good natured.
- They have a very compact and proportionate physique.
- These goats are very alert.
- Their animated behaviour provides a great source of entertainment.
- Although the breed is small in size, the amount of muscle on the structure of this breed makes it a good meat providing breed.
- The Kinder goats also produce a large quantity of milk for its size.
- The level of butterfat in the milk of the Kinders is high, making it very nutritious.
- The breed is highly productive, often having multiple births, which include quadruplets as well.
- Easy to maintain and manage.

*Cons of this breed:*
- You need to be highly prepared during the kidding season.
- You need to watch what they eat as they are susceptible to digestive issues.
- They love to climb, which makes fencing a challenge.

# 4. Pygora Goat

A Pygora goat, as the name itself suggests, is a cross between a Pygmy goat and an Angora. This goat is mostly grown for its quality of fleece. Pygora goats are usually kept as pets because of their calm and docile nature. In addition to that, they are also extremely good looking goats. Usually, the weight of a Pygora goat depends entirely upon the gender and the age of the goat. At birth they are about 5 pounds in weight and can go up to 95 pounds when they are adults.

The quality of fleece produced by these goats is excellent. It is usually used in clothing and several artefacts. Artists make use of Pygora fleece for weaving, tapestries, crocheting, spindling and knitting.
The first generation pygoras produced by breeding a Pygmy with an Angora are not considered pure Pygora goats. Only when the first generation is bred with another Pygora, it is considered a pure Pygora. Basically, a pure Pygora is defined as a goat that has less than 75% of an Angora or Pygmy history.

*History of the Pygora:*
 In the year 1987, a Pygora Goat Breeders association was formed. The objective of this association was to promote the Pygora goat that was created by Katherine Jorgensen from Oregon city. Today, any Pygora that has less than 75% of the ancestry of a Pygmy or Angora can be registered under this association.

### Pros of this breed:
- It is compact in size.
- It can be milked to produce about 1 litre of milk every day.
- It is a valuable show animal.
- It is a good natured breed.

·      The breed is valued for its ability to produce fleece. There are three kinds of fleece that are available. Type A fleece consists of fibres that are 6 inches or more in length. Type B fleece is between 3 to 6 inches in length and the Type C fleece is usually between 1 to 3 inches in length.

·      The breed comes in several colors including red, brown, white black and grey. There are also mixed colors that are available.

### Cons of the breed:

·      The maintenance of the coat is quite hard.

·      Fleecing requires a lot of time and expertise.

Besides these pure bred pygmy goats, there are several mini versions of regular goat breeds that are available. The Mini fainting goats and the mini Oberhalsi are the most popular ones of them all. Whenever you are choosing a mini goat, be clear of the purpose of the goat, so that you can bring the right breed home.

# Chapter 4. Pygmy goats

## A Brief History of the Pygmy Goat

The pygmy goat was originally called the Cameroon Dwarf Goat. The goat (in its pure form, gray in color with black stockings and very small in size) is mostly restricted to the West African countries. Similar forms of Pygmy goats also occur in all of northern Africa, in the southwestern African countries, and also in East Africa. However, what we call the Cameroon Dwarf Goat is the one that we are concerned with, and have here now in the West. It is the species that actually came from the former French Cameroon area.

The little Cameroon goats were exported from Africa to zoos in Sweden and Germany where they were on display as exotic animals. From there they made their way to England, Canada, and the United States. In 1959 the Rhue family (California) and the Catskill Game Farm (New York) received the first documented shipments of Pygmy goats from Sweden. These original animals were purchased from German zoos and through a complicated arrangement of transporting them to Sweden, a country that was on the approved list for imports by the United States Department of Agriculture, they were allowed into the United States. Offspring of these animals, as well as earlier imports, were sold to zoos, medical research, and to some private individuals.

By the 1970's, interest in the Pygmy goat began to grow to the point that registries for the Pygmy goats were established to define breed type and to encourage the breeding of pure Pygmies. In 1975 the incorporated National Pygmy Goat Association was formed.

In the 1980's the Pygmy goat population began to experience a significant increase, as did membership in the National Pygmy Goat Association. Today, as the number of goats increases, so do the number of shows in which they may be exhibited.

## Some Considerations with Raising Pygmy Goats

Like all farm animals, goats are creatures of habit. Be sure you have the time to give your animals regular care before you decide to purchase them, or you will be disappointed in the results.

Before you actually buy a goat, check city or township regulations. Find out if you live in an area where animals can be raised. Some towns have strict zoning regulations. If the above conditions are fine, and you have made a real commitment to raising goats, there is one last thing to consider – space requirements. Will there be adequate housing or room to erect other buildings should your project expand? Is there enough land to have an outside yard?

## Selecting Your Pygmy Goat

If you are interested in breeding and raising goats for show and sale, purchase registered animals. If your main interest is having a goat for a pet, you may want to consider purchasing a wether (castrated male), as they are usually less expensive than registered females. A goat bought for a pet should be friendly. Whatever you decide to purchase, Pygmy goats are very sociable and are happier in a herd atmosphere or with another goat as a friend. A doe and wether or two wethers is a good place to start. Bucks are not considered suitable as pets and should only be purchased as a breeding animal by owners of several breedable does. Owners with only a few does should consider taking them to Pygmy goat breeders in their area for breeding.

Beginners should start with a kid at least 10 to 12 weeks old. At this age they are more ready to be independent of their dams than a younger kid. Be careful if taking a kid to bottle raise. Be sure it is started well on a bottle and be absolutely sure you have the time and skill to devote to properly raise a bottle fed kid. Starting with a young goat gives you an opportunity to get acquainted with goats and their habits during growth. You can learn the management phases of caring for goats and what to do at kidding time before the goat is old enough to kid. Healthy older animals can make great starter goats too. Don't pass up a nice adult goat. A calmer sturdier adult may actually be a better choice in many situations.

In making your choice, consider:
- Reputation of the person from whom you intend to obtain your Pygmy goat
- Physical appearance and condition of the goat you intend to purchase.
- Show and health records of the goat's ancestors.
- 

It's always a good idea to talk with the Pygmy goat breeders in your area before purchasing an animal. Most areas also have local Pygmy goat clubs to help you in locating just the right goat and are an excellent source of information and assistance with questions and problems.

### *The Doe*
**The Doe**: Female goat, the foundation of a herd.

**Purpose:** Primarily as a breeder, but wait until she is at least 12 months of age before having her bred. She should always represent a good example of the Pygmy Goat breed standard; even when breeding is not initially intended, most does will bear young at some time in their lives. Estrus Period of heat, which cycles about every 18-21 days. Pygmy does will usually breed year round.

**Her General Needs:** A good quality hay should always be available. Water should be clean and always available. In winter warm water is appreciated. For food 1 to 2 cups (¼ to ½ pound) of grain a day divided between morning and night. For pregnant does, during the last four weeks and when lactating does should have grain doubled. Salt Trace mineral should be always available. Deworming should be performed at least 3 to 4 times a year. Worm in the last month of pregnancy and again just before or right after kidding with a wormer safe for pregnant does; this protects the kids (check with your veterinarian).

Hoof Trimming should be performed at least every 4 to 6 weeks but more often if needed. Vaccinations follow a recommended schedule. In the last months of pregnancy, tetanus and enterotoxemia vaccinations are important; the immunized doe imparts immunity to the young through colostrum (first milk).

Housing should be clean, dry and draft free with a stall available a week or so before kidding where the doe may be quiet and relaxed. Fencing should be 4 to 6 feet high, if rail or board fencing is used, make sure kids cannot go under or through. The fencing should be strong enough to keep the goats in and other animals out (e.g. dogs, coyotes, etc.). Horns may be kept for aesthetic reasons or she may be disbudded.

### The Wether
**The Wether**: A male of less than desirable breeding quality that has been castrated. Castration is recommended between 4 weeks and 6 months (3 months is average).

**Purpose**: Primarily as a pet, he also makes a fine companion for other animals, such as a buck or horse, and may be used as a heat detector for does. The Whether is more effeminate as a direct result of castration with little or no beard, shorter hair growth, and feminine horn growth - he may also grow larger in size.

**His General Needs:** A good quality hay should always be available. Water should be clean and always available. In winter warm water is appreciated. Do not overfeed him grain - probably not more than ½ to 1 cup per day divided between morning and night. Salt Trace mineral should always be readily available.

Deworming must be performed at least 3 to 4 times a year. Hoof Trimming should be at least every 4 to 6 weeks but more often if necessary. For vaccinations, follow a recommended schedule, but tetanus protection is important.

Housing should be clean, dry, and draft free so the animal can escape bad weather. Fencing should be 4 to 6 feet - strong enough and high enough to keep the goat in and dogs or other animals out - tethering a goat is dangerous and is not advised. Horns may be kept for aesthetic reasons or he may be disbudded.

## *Recognizing The Pygmy Goat*
Learn the names of the different parts of the animal and their comparative importance in judging. After you become familiar with the Pygmy, you will be in a much better position to select an animal and know whether it is good, very good or excellent.

The Pygmy Goat is genetically small, cobby, and compact. Full -barreled and well-muscled, the body circumference in relation to height and weight is proportionately greater than that of other breeds. Mature does measure between 16 and 22 inches at the withers. Head and legs are shorter than in other breeds but should be balanced in relation to body length. Genetic hornlessness (polled) is considered a disqualifying fault. However, disbudded (dehorned) or horned goats are acceptable.

## *Housing*
You will need some type of simple shelter for your animal. It need not be elaborate, but should be capable of providing shelter from sun, rain, and wind. It should be dry, free from drafts, and clean. Goats, more than most other animals, are very picky about clean, dry living conditions. A small shed about 8 X 10 feet will adequately house two adult animals. If you do not provide some shelter, your goat will be more likely to have respiratory difficulties or even pneumonia. Use a bedding such as sawdust, shavings or straw, and change the bedding regularly.

Goats can be outside most of the time as long as they have a building to go into for shelter from the sun, rain, wind, ice, and snow. An attached outside enclosure with at least 4 foot high fencing will provide fresh air and exercise. The area must be fenced to keep out stray dogs or other predators. Be sure to use a good gate fastener, as goats learn to open many gates.

During the winter months the housing area needs to be dry and free of drafts. Buildings with heavy condensation are particularly harmful to goats. Keep their bedded area clean by removing the manure daily. (Use the manure on your field or garden.) Also, the hay, grain and water must be placed so that goat manure will not get into them. Goats are very particular about clean, fresh water, just as they are about dry housing. To save labor, time and perhaps building costs, plan to store the hay needed by your goats on the same level as the housing. Also, store the grain close to the place where it will be fed, but be careful it is secure from dampness, other animals and your goats.

During cold, damp weather, goat kids usually need special consideration. To prevent them having colds and coughs, be certain you keep the shelter dry and free of drafts. An enclosed area in a larger building will work well for the mother and her young kids, and for the kids after they have been weaned and separated from the mother. Again, to emphasize, dry, draft - free quarters are very important.

Goats love to climb and jump and appreciate "toys" in their outside yards. Items such as large rocks, a picnic table, or a constructed platform encourages them to climb, helps build muscle and encourages proper leg movement.

# Feeding

The feed requirements for Pygmy goats vary with age, sex, health, climate, and pregnancy. Different feeding practices are necessary in order to provide the needed nutrients for each goat's individual needs.

Knowing what to feed your goats is just as important as knowing when to feed them. The ideal ration must be formulated and fed so that it will support optimum production, minimize nutrition related problems and be economical to handle and feed.

The nutrients of primary importance are water, energy as measured by total digestible nutrients (TDN), protein as indicated by crude or digestible protein, minerals (especially salt, calcium and phosphorus, as these are the most critical minerals to maintain at proper levels), and vitamins, with vitamin A being of primary concern.

### Feed Requirements:
**Water:** Water is essential to successful goat production and should be available at all times. Further, its quality is of importance, as goats will not drink stagnant, poor quality water. If they are forced to do so, production

will be reduced greatly. As for average quantity needed, goats generally require one gallon for every four pounds of air-dry feed consumed.

**Energy:** Major sources of energy for goats are hay, silage, and pasture. Grains such as corn, barley, milo, wheat, and oats are used to raise the energy level of the ration. Protein supplements and grains are high in TDN, Total Digestible Nutrients (70 -80%), hay is intermediate (30-55%), and silage very low (10-30%). Hay or silage may be self-fed or hand-fed daily at frequent intervals. Grain should be fed according to the goats needs but not to exceed half the diet. Inadequate energy intake will result in a slowing or stopping of growth, loss of weight, and increased mortality, especially in pregnant or nursing does. Resistance to disease and parasitism is also increased.

**Protein:** The amount of protein in goat rations is much more important than protein quality. Regardless of the type of protein fed, it is changed almost completely by bacterial action when it reaches the rumen, the largest chamber of a four-stomach digestion. (However, this is not true in very young goats since there is little or no rumen activity.) Bacteria in the rumen take the nitrogen protein of the proteins and remake bacterial protozoal protein.

As the bacteria and protozoa die and are moved along to the true stomach and small intestine, they are attacked by normal digestive juices and are broken down to simple compounds called amino acids, which are absorbed and utilized by goats. For this reason, goats can utilize food protein and non-protein nitrogen in their diets. Properly harvested legume hays, while intermediate in protein content (12-16%), when used as a complete ration will provide adequate protein for most goats. Oil such as soybean meal, linseed meal, and peanut meal contain large amounts of protein (35-40%) and are excellent protein supplements for goats. Soybean oil meal, in addition, is particularly palatable and will stimulate appetite.

**Salt:** Salt is known to have many regulatory functions in the body and should be made available at all times. When goats are deprived of salt, feed consumption and water intake are decreased. Growth rate will be reduced. Animals desiring salt may chew on wood, lick dirt and possibly consume poisonous plants that would not normally be eaten. Loose salt, rather than salt blocks, should be provided in a dry location. Goats bite at salt blocks rather than lick, and teeth may be broken. Use of a complete sheep and goat trace mineral salt mix purchased in your area will adjust for local conditions.

**Calcium:** Most pasture legume hays and range forages contain adequate levels of calcium, while grains are generally somewhat deficient in this mineral. Finely ground limestone and dicalcium phosphate are good sources of calcium for supplementation. However, don't over feed; excessive calcium may be more of a problem than a deficiency.

**Phosphorus:** Matured pasture and range plants are quite low in phosphorus content while grains are relatively high. Forages containing less than 0.16% phosphorus are considered deficient for goats. Stored phosphorus can be used to some extent by goats. Steamed bonemeal or dicalcium phosphate may be used as phosphorus supplements.

**Vitamins:** Mature goats are known to require the fat soluble vitamins A, D, E and K, but do not need sources of the B vitamins since these are synthesized in adequate amounts by rumen microorganisms. Normal goat rations are adequate in all of the fat soluble vitamins with the exception of vitamin A in old hay or dry summer pastures. You may want to make a special effort to supplement this vitamin. Warning: Vitamins A, D, and E can be toxic if overdosed.

**Trace Minerals:** Many other minerals are needed for proper growth. One way to guarantee a source of these trace minerals is to provide trace mineralized sheep and goat salt. Some regions are naturally deficient in iodine and selenium, both of which are necessary for good health. (Everyone should contact their county extension agent or veterinarian to see if additional selenium is needed for their area of the country).

Therefore, they must be supplemented via the diet, with mineral mixes, or by injection. Sheep and goat trace mineral loose salt, that contains both iodine and selenium, should be made available free choice to your goats. Loose salt is preferable to a salt block and should be fed from a box or feeder that is protected from the weather.

A salt feeder separate from their hay and grain should be used. Without adequate amounts of selenium and Vitamin E, goats are susceptible to White Muscle Disease, which is often fatal. An injectable form of selenium and Vitamin E is available through your veterinarian and can be used along with the selenium salt mix in severely deficient areas of the country.

## *Kids*
Kids must get colostrum milk (the first milk) from their mothers within the first hour or sooner after birth. This first milk from the mother is important

because it contains disease-fighting antibodies, vitamins, protein, energy, and minerals, all of which help the kid get a good start in life. Colostrum acts as a mild laxative, too, which helps clean out the kid's digestive system.

Pygmy does are usually excellent mothers, and often the mother of quadruplets will successfully raise all four babies herself. Occasions do arise, however, when the newborn kids must be bottle-fed entirely, or at least supplemented.

If circumstances are such that the kid(s) is/are unable to nurse its/their mother, the mother's colostrum or frozen colostrum must be given by bottle within the first hour after birth. The kid's digestive tract will only be able to absorb the antibodies from the colostrum for the first 12 hours after birth, so feeding colostrum as soon as possible after birth is extremely important. After the first 3 days the best formula to feed baby goats is goat milk. Fresh milk from the mother or your other Pygmy does is the ideal, since Pygmy milk is higher in butterfat content than dairy goats.

WARNING: Raw, unpasteurized, fresh goat milk could cause CAE Caprine Arthritis Encephalitis. If you are unable to obtain fresh goat milk or fresh cow milk (Jersey cow milk works well), then get a goat milk or lamb milk replacer. Don't use cow milk replacer, as it is too low in butter fat content to meet the needs of a growing Pygmy kid. Feeding utensils should be thoroughly sanitized after each feeding in order to prevent digestive upsets and to help guard the kid's health.

Here are some general feeding recommendations for your bottle-fed or bottle supplemented kids:

1. Increase the quantity of milk gradually and according to the kid's size and capacity.

2. Keep the feedings on a routine schedule spaced evenly about the same number of hours apart and at the same times each day.

3. During the first week offer the kids good quality alfalfa hay and make water and salt available.

4. Continue to feed milk or allow the kids to nurse, but also offer a dry starter grain mixture when the kids are around 3 weeks old. The mixture should contain no less than 14% protein, including corn, oats, or some other high-energy feed, and should be fortified with minerals and vitamins.

**5**. At 10 to 12 weeks old, when the kids are eating grain and hay, and drinking water, weaning may be started by gradually decreasing a little at a time the amount of milk fed. Always make feeding changes gradually over a period of a week or 10 days for goats of any age. Doing this helps to prevent enterotoxemia and digestive problems.

### Growing Goats

After the young goat is weaned, provide a basic diet of roughage in the form of good quality alfalfa hay supplemented with grain in the form of a commercial sweet feed or dairy ration. One cup, preferably divided into two feedings, should be fed daily.

Body condition will tell you how much grain to feed a young, growing Pygmy goat. You should be able to feel the ribs and along the edges of the loin of a growing yearling. If you cannot feel the ribs and along the sides of the loin, you are feeding too much grain. The idea is to feed the young animal enough grain for rapid growth but not enough to make it fat.

### Pregnant Does

Pregnant does should be fed enough to provide for the developing fetus without allowing the doe to become fat. Good quality alfalfa hay, plus 1 cup of grain a day, should be adequate for most does. More grain will be needed, however, if the doe is thin.

About 3-4 weeks before the doe is expected to give birth, gradually increase the grain feeding to about 2-3 cups per day in two feedings. Do this regardless of body condition. This will help prevent ketosis and other problems that can occur near kidding time.

Does that are nursing one or more kids will require 3-4 cups of grain a day and high quality legume hay free choice. Make sure that she has access to adequate quantities of fresh clean water at all times but make sure the kids cannot drown if they accidentally jump into the bucket. Using two or three small buckets will provide ample water but the buckets will tip over easily if a kid falls into one of them. Flat, round dog dishes or plastic dishpans make good water bowls, as they are too shallow for kids to drown in but don't tip easily.

During winter months, when water will freeze, offer warm water often, at least two times a day but more frequently if possible, or place buckets on heaters designed to keep water from freezing. Be careful that the heating element is not accessible to kids that could sleep on them and accidentally become burned. Make sure all cords are out of reach of inquisitive goats.

Remember, the doe has to take in enough quality feed to support not only her own body's needs but to supply adequate milk production for growing kids.

### Grain Mixtures

There are a variety of formulated goat feeds on the market depending on the nutritional needs of your goat. They vary in protein content. In most cases a mix of corn, oats, and barley (called COB) is readily available and is adequate for most goats except pregnant or nursing does or breeding bucks.

## Management Practices

There are several management skills and practices you should learn. A brief description of the more important ones follows.

### Foot Care

Like your own fingernails, the hooves of all goats need to be trimmed from time to time. Since the goat has no way of doing this for itself, you must take care of trimming the hooves as needed. However, the more often you trim, the less you have to do each time. It's a good idea to check each animal once a month.

The idea is to trim excess growth from the toes and to make the sole of the foot flat so your goat can stand straight on its feet with the hooves in the proper position and not bent unnaturally. Also, untrimmed or poorly trimmed hooves cause a goat much discomfort and can even result in serious lameness, foot rot, or splayed toes. This is especially true of pregnant does. Check with a goat breeder in your area for assistance in learning how to trim hooves properly.

Use a small hand pruner to trim. If possible, secure your animal against a fence or wall or on a stanchion. If you are right-handed, stand on the right side of the goat to trim the front feet. When working on the left hoof, reach across the animal and brace her body against yours. If you are left-handed, stand on the left side and use the same procedure.

Work on one toe at a time. Always cut from heel to toe and trim the bottom of the hoof so that it is parallel with the top. With the first cut, remove the outer wall of the hoof. Then level the heel and sole to make the hoof level. You may need to trim some extra off the tip of the toe in order to improve the shape of the foot. Also, check between the two hooves near the heels an overgrown hoof, or goats with certain hoof conformation defects, may tend to grow extra hoof into this space. It will cause splaying of the hooves and can become quite uncomfortable for the goat. Trim this excess growth until it is even with the normal inside wall of the hoof. It is seldom necessary to remove much of the sole. If it is, trim in thin slices and stop when the sole turns a pinkish color; if you do not, you may draw blood. If you should nick the hoof and have it start bleeding, apply 7% iodine, Kopertox, or blood stop powder or liquid to the area. With a clean rag or paper towel, apply pressure until the bleeding has stopped. Make sure that the goat's tetanus toxoid booster is up to date.

When you finish the first toe, begin on the other. Be careful to trim both toes so that when the foot is placed on the ground the toes will be the same length. When you trim the rear feet, stand to the rear. Bring the goat's leg up, bending at the knee and being careful not to pull it out to the side. Trim in the same manner as the front feet.

### Goat Identification
All goats should either be tattooed or microchipped, whether they are to be registered or not. Being able to positively identify your goat can save many problems as time goes on.

### Tattooing
Tattoo kits for goats contain tattoo pliers and a series of letters and numbers. The letters and numbers are small enough that they fit well in the goat's ear or tail webbing. Your county extension agent, veterinarian or an experienced goat breeder in your area can assist you in tattooing. They can help you locate the equipment you will need as well as show you how to do the job correctly.

There is another method of tattooing, with an electric tattooer, on the abdomen where the rear leg joins the body. The equipment for this type of tattooing is expensive, but you may be able to locate a local Pygmy goat club or breeder that has this equipment and who may do belly tattooing for a nominal fee.

### Microchipping
With this system, a tiny microchip is injected under the skin or tail webbing which contains a one of a kind identification number. The microchips are so small that they fit through a hypodermic needle. When a scanner is run over the goat in the area where the microchip has been injected, the microchip number activates in the scanner, and the identification number appears. Scanners and microchips are commercially available from several sources; your county extension agent, veterinarian or experienced goat breeder can provide you with contact information.

## Measuring

In order to be registered, Pygmy goats over a year old must be measured; this requirement does not apply for those who are one year old or younger. The measurements are the height at the withers and the length of the front cannon bone.

A good way to measure a goat's height at the withers is to place the animal on a flat, level board. Supply a bucket of grain at a level where the goat can eat while standing in a normal posture. Holding the head high will tend to raise the withers and increase the height. Holding the head low will decrease the height measurement.

Use a yardstick and a right-angle device such as a T-square, Triangle, or Carpenter's square. With one hand, hold the top of the yardstick straight up and down, about an inch in back of the front legs. If you have trouble holding the yardstick perpendicular, tape another right-angle to its base. Place the right-angle device against the yardstick. Grasp both devices firmly, making sure both edges remain parallel to each other. Then slide the right-angle device down along the yardstick until it touches the withers, which is the high point of the goat's back, just above the front legs. (This may take practice).

As soon as the device touches the withers, be prepared for the goat to move. Press the right-angle device to the yardstick and, keeping them together, pull them away. Then read the number at the point where the right-angle edge touches the yardstick.

To measure the length of the cannon bone, it is easiest on both you and your goat if it is eating. It is best to have someone hold the leg in position while you measure. With one hand, bend the foreleg. With the other hand, hold the calipers against the cannon bone and adjust the device until it touches the outside edges of the knee and pastern joints.

Pull the entire device away and measure the distance between the two right angles on the measuring stick. Repeat your measuring several times to make sure you have measured accurately.

## Disbudding (Dehorning)

Pygmy goats may be shown with or without horns, but disbudding is strongly suggested. Like many other animals, goats establish a "pecking" order and sometimes butt each other around. Horns can rip up udders and frequently get caught in fences. Pygmy goats are not usually aggressive, but horns can be dangerous for your children who are at "horn level."

Although judges will not fault a Pygmy for having horns in a sanctioned show, disbudding may be mandatory in some areas for 4-H exhibitors. Basically, it is much easier to handle a hornless animal. For these reasons, it's best to dehorn your goats. Disbudding should be done before they are three weeks old (bucks at about one week old, does at about two weeks old). The longer you wait, the more difficult the job becomes and the better the chance that the horns will grow back.

Goats have nerve ends and a blood supply in their horns; sawing the horns off after the animal is grown is a shock to the animal's nervous system and can result in death. Have your veterinarian remove horns, as animals should be anesthetized for this surgical procedure.

All Pygmy goats will grow horns, unless you disbud the kids (remove the horn buds). If a Pygmy goat is naturally hornless (polled) this is a disqualifying fault in the show ring and the animal cannot be registered, even if purebred
.

The first job, then, is to find out whether the kid is horned or polled. You will need to do this early, at 7 to 10 days of age. Here's how:

**1**. Check the growth pattern of the hair over where the horns should be on the poll. Horned goats will have a swirl pattern over each horn bud. Polled goats will have a straight pattern over the area and a single swirl pattern in the center of the head.

**2**. Move the skin over the area back and forth. The skin will be tight if the kid is a horned goat. Free movement of the skin over the area indicates that the kid is polled.

If you have never disbudded before, have an experienced person show you how and help you the first few times.

There are several methods of disbudding a goat. However, caustic sticks or pastes are difficult and dangerous to handle and, therefore, are not recommended. The quickest and easiest method is the electric disbudding iron with a goat tip. This can be purchased from a goat dairy supply firm or veterinary catalog. It looks like a soldering iron with the tip sawed off. Disbudding a goat kid with a disbudding iron is a task to not be taken lightly.

The necessary heat of the iron, the pressure to be applied with the iron over the horn buds, the time necessary to apply the pressure, and the technique used to pop the bud loose all require the practice and experience

34

gained under the tutelage of an experienced goat disbudder. A beginner should not attempt this procedure without such guidance and assistance. After the buds are removed, apply an antibiotic spray or liquid to each area where the buds were formerly located. The kid should get a shot of tetanus antitoxin at this time to prevent the chance of tetanus. Allow the kid to nurse on its mother, reintroducing the kids rear end first to its mother so she is not confused by the smell of the burnt horns. In the case of bottle fed babies, have a bottle of milk handy and give it to the kid at once. This will help him forget the discomfort quickly.

If you are unable to purchase an electric disbudding iron and cannot find someone who can help you, take your kid to a veterinarian who is experienced with goats. He can disbud your goat for you or show you how to do it effectively. Again, tetanus antitoxin should be given at the time you disbud to prevent tetanus.

## *Castrating*

Male kids should be castrated (have their testicles removed), if they are to be kept or sold as pets. Kids can be castrated as early as 4 weeks old and up to any age. There is no suggested ideal time but 3 months is a good average. The testicles must be descended into the scrotum before castration can be done. A castrated male goat is called a wether. There are three methods used in castrating: (1) use of an elastrator, (2) use of the emasculatome, and (3) use of a knife, razor blade, or other sharp cutting instrument. Someone who has had experience with one of these methods should be present to help perform the procedure and teach you how to do a castration or your veterinarian can assist you.

Kids need to be given a tetanus antitoxin shot at the time of castration to prevent tetanus.

The elastrator is an instrument for expanding a special rubber ring so it can be placed above the testicles. In using this method, you expand the ring and slip it over the testicles and below the rudimentary teats, being sure both testicles are present before releasing the ring. The dried testicles will usually slough off in ten days to two weeks. This method should only be used on younger animals. If used during fly season, be sure to check the animal often for maggot invasion of the scrotal tissue. After the scrotum falls off, be sure to check that both testicles were removed and the animal is truly a wether.

The emasculatome, or Burdizzo, is a heavy, long-handled, cord-crushing instrument. It is placed above each testicle, but below the rudimentary teats. Crush each cord separately and leave the instrument on for about 10-15 seconds. Do the second cord below the first one. The scrotum remains on the animal but the testicles atrophy because the blood supply can no longer get to them.

This is another procedure that should only be attempted under the supervision of an experienced operator of this equipment. If for whatever reason you choose to have your goat castrated by cutting the scrotum to expose the testicles, this procedure is best left for an experienced professional. Although a surgical castration is best left to a veterinarian, some accomplished breeders perform this procedure themselves. This do-it-yourself castration method is not recommended for home use. Remember, your veterinarian will be able to castrate your male kids for a small fee. When cutting instruments or the elastrator are used, it is best to do the job before fly season and preferably before warm weather arrives. Otherwise, check frequently to be sure no maggot invasions occur and there is no infection.

# Health Care
### *Recognizing When Something is Wrong*
Regular, careful observation is needed to keep your goats healthy. The ability to observe, in fact, is the most essential attribute of a good herdsman. Animals can "tell" you when they are sick. It is essential that you understand each animal's normal behavior to be able to identify when something is wrong. The signs that you should monitor every day:

- General attitude alert and inquisitive
- Appetite the goat should be interested in food at almost any time
- Cudding at certain times of the day your goat should chew her cud
- Eyes and nose bright eyes and no nasal discharge
- Coat clean and glossy
- Feces droppings are firm and pelleted
- Breathing regular and unlabored
- Gait steady with all feet taking weight as the goat walks
- 

In order to notice any deviation from normal, it is essential to be familiar with the normal behavior. There are some signs to look for that may help you recognize when your goat is not feeling well:

- Tends to stay away from other goats and/or you
- Has a distressed or depressed expression in the eyes
- Looks dull and listless

- Does not want to move
- Grinds teeth
- Breathes in a quick, shallow fashion or coughs a lot
- Has no appetite, is not interested in its food
- Urinates frequently
- Tries to urinate but is unable to do so, especially in wethers
- Exhibits a changed color and consistency in the feces, i.e. scours (diarrhea)
- Has a temperature above normal
- Shows drastic change from normal habits and behavior
- Head pressing, presses head against wall or fence
- 

Good management and careful observation will help you keep your goats free of disease. Such practices will also help you spot problems early, when the most can usually be done to help the goat. The temperature has a wide range variation that is influenced by environment and the goat's activity. A temperature taken first thing in the morning on an inactive animal will be at the low end of the range. A temperature taken on a hot day when you've just chased the goat around the barn will be at the high end of the scale. Temperature must be looked at along with other symptoms when reporting it to your veterinarian.

Preventive medicine is extremely important for our domestic animals. Confinement rearing of animals, even when large pastures and spacious barns are available, results in exposure to bacteria, viruses and parasites. For a well-balanced and effective herd health program, it is necessary to use vaccinations, vitamin and mineral supplements and parasiticides. The herd health program should include the use of vaccines for tetanus on a short term basis (tetanus antitoxin), tetanus for long term immunization (tetanus toxoid), and prevention for enterotoxemia (Clostridium Perfringens Type C&D).

Short-term tetanus is used when exposure to possible tetanus is increased by an animal having an open wound. Examples as to when it would be suggested are at birth, dehorning, and castration.

Long term tetanus immunization is given in two initial doses to kids and then a booster is given annually; also preferably given to does 3 to 4 weeks prior to kidding so the immunity will be passed to her kids through the colostrum. Enterotoxemia (overeating disease) immunization is given in two initial doses to kids and then a booster is given annually; also preferably to does 3 to 4 weeks prior to kidding so the immunity is passed to her kids.

# Vaccination Schedule

This is a suggested schedule and each goat owner should work with a veterinarian to develop a herd health program.

Kids born to non-immunized does and colostrum deprived kids receive the following:
- 1 dose of Clostridium perfringens C&D vaccine (this is of questionable value at birth)
- 1 dose of Tetanus antitoxin (150 -250 units)
- 150-250 units of Tetanus antitoxin when dehorning or castrating, or in cases of puncture wounds. Antitoxin remains in the body for about 2 weeks, then follow the 5 and 9 week schedule below.
-

Kids born to immunized does receive the following:
150-250 units of Tetanus antitoxin when dehorning or castrating, or in cases of puncture wounds. Antitoxin remains in the body for about 2 weeks.
- 5-6 Weeks: 1 dose of Clostridium perfringens C&D vaccine
  1 dose of Tetanus toxoid
- 9-10 Weeks: 1 dose of Clostridium perfringens C&D vaccine
  1 dose of Tetanus toxoid
- Yearly boosters: 1 dose of Clostridium perfringens C&D vaccine
  1 dose of Tetanus toxoid
- Does 3-4 Weeks Prior To Kidding:
-

Immunizing the doe prior to kidding will allow transfer of antibodies to the kids through the colostrum.
- 1 dose Clostridium perfringens C&D vaccine
- 1 dose Tetanus toxoid
-

Clostridium perfringens C&D and Tetanus toxoid is now produced in a combined vaccine; follow label directions for dosage. If, however, the vaccines are purchased separately, do not combine the drugs in the same syringe, but give the injections separately.

Directions on the bottle must be followed when giving medications as to the amount of dose and how to give the medication. Read all labels on medication bottles every time you give a medication and follow directions. Be sure to check the expiration date shown on the label. Do not vaccinate pregnant does with a live virus unless approved by a veterinarian.
Any medication that is given to an animal by injection has the ability to cause an anaphylactic reaction (allergic reaction) to the drug. Always

watch your goats for 10-15 minutes after giving medication and observe for symptoms of a reaction:
- Restlessness
- Difficulty breathing (dyspnea)
   Loss of muscle function (unable to stand)
- Seizures
-

If a reaction occurs take your animal to the nearest veterinarian IMMEDIATELY!!! This is a medical emergency. Epinephrine is the drug used to counteract an anaphylactic reaction. If you have epinephrine, give ¼cc to kids and ½cc to adult goats subcutaneously (under the skin) and follow up by taking the animal to the nearest veterinarian.
Talk to your veterinarian about assisting you in implementing a herd health program and always check with your veterinarian before immunizing or using any drugs.

# Disease
Even with preventative medicine and observation, disease cannot always be avoided. Following are some of the illnesses you may encounter. Watch your goat for signs of health problems which can develop rapidly. If it acts strangely or shows other signs of difficulty, have someone who knows goats look at your animal immediately. If there is any uncertainty about its condition, ask your veterinarian for help.

### *Parasites:*
Parasites, both internal and external, are probably the most important health hazard you must deal with.*Internal Parasites*:

A heavy parasite infestation causes poor health and sometimes death. The eggs of parasites are passed out of the goat's body with the feces, and can survive for many months in the barn or pasture. As long as they survive, infection can occur. Exposure to dry air and sunlight helps destroy parasite eggs. Young animals and poorly nourished goats will be affected the most by parasite infestations. The common internal parasites include lung worms, stomach worms and tape worms.

These are ways you can help control the development of internal parasites. A regular deworming program is essential for good health and proper growth. Animals should be dewormed at least three to four times a year, rotating worm medications to achieve a higher degree of effectiveness. Worming should be done two weeks prior to kidding (with a medication proven safe to be used during pregnancy) and again immediately before or just after kidding, before breeding, with the other one or two times spaced throughout the year. Kids are wormed at four to six weeks old and then with the rest of the herd. Consult your veterinarian or county extension office for the best methods to use. Your veterinarian can perform fecal examinations to identify the type of parasite involved and determine how efficacious the treatments are. Maintain a good level of nutrition. Prevent manure from getting into the feed and water. Place all feeders and water buckets high enough to prevent such contamination. Confine the goats about a day after deworming them in order to keep a load of parasites from being dumped onto the pasture.

Watch your animals at times of stress. Often, you will need to deworm the kids just before or at the time of weaning. Check with your veterinarian for help in identifying parasites that are causing trouble. Use the proper treatment. Doing the wrong thing only makes the situation worse.

### *External Parasites* :
Watch your animals for external parasites lice, ticks, domestic flies, screwworms, and fly maggots. These are all very harmful to your goat. To prevent the spread of such parasites, inspect your goat when you buy it. Also, reduce the fly problem by keeping the shelter and pen sanitary. Still, there may be times when you have to take extra measures. Sprays and insecticide dusts and liquids can be useful. But keep in mind that all insecticides are poisonous and must be used with caution. Do not let them come into contact with feed, water or the containers of feed and water. Wash your hands thoroughly after using insecticides. Contact your veterinarian for advice before using any insecticides if your goat is thin, sick, or nursing kids. Lice are a common parasite on goats. They are particularly active in the winter when the goats have their heaviest coats.

Besides being a source of constant discomfort and irritation to the goats, a heavy louse infestation can produce a severe anemia in their hosts. Animals should be inspected frequently for lice and should be treated in the late fall before being confined to the barn for the winter. Dusting your goats approximately every 6 to 10 days for one month with a delousing powder that is safe to use on lactating cattle should control the problem. This should be followed by light applications of the powder once every four to six weeks. Goats should also be deloused on returning home from a show or fair before being put back in their barn. Remember to check with your veterinarian before using any medication on your animals.

### *Coccidiosis*
Coccidia of goats is a disease caused by microscopic protozoan organisms that live in the cells of the intestinal lining and are shed in the feces.

Infection occurs when kids ingest contaminated feed or water. Goat coccidia is species specific, meaning it can't infect other animals. The symptoms can vary from loss of appetite and slight, short-lived diarrhea to severe cases involving severe diarrhea, loss of weight and appetite, dull appearance, and dehydration. Death can occur without proper treatment. Stress produced at weaning, when feed is changed, and when animals are moved can be a trigger for producing the disease symptoms. The protozoan is normally found in the intestine of all goats.

Diagnosis is made through fecal examination under a microscope. Goats that survive a disease outbreak are usually immune to future problems. Prevention includes 1) good sanitation, 2) keeping water and feed pans free from fecal contamination, 3) reducing crowding and stress, and 4) isolation of goats with diarrhea. Several products that can be added to feed, water, or salt are used for treatment and control. Consult with your veterinarian for diagnosis and treatment.

## *Pneumonia*
Pneumonia is one of the most common diseases found in goats. Healthy animals may carry the bacteria, viruses, or lung parasites that can cause pneumonia. However, the disease usually develops due to stress from chilling, poor feeding, parasitism, or prolonged exposure, along with the presence of these infectious agents.

Barns that are poorly ventilated with a strong ammonia odor in the air and damp bedding are unhealthy for goats.
The disease is characterized by fever, persistent coughing, rapid or labored breathing, and refusal to eat. Later, the animal becomes depressed and may have a discharge from the eyes and nose. Sometimes older goats die without showing any symptoms.

Prevention is the best cure. It is important to prevent conditions that would predispose an animal to the disease.

1. Warm, dry, draft free housing should be provided.
2. Young kids should be protected from wind and rain.
3. Parasites should be controlled.
4. Housing should be properly ventilated.
5. Animals should be fed and managed properly.

Prompt action is necessary for effective treatment. Sick animals should be separated and a veterinarian contacted for diagnosis and treatment.
## *Tetanus (Lockjaw)*

The tetanus organism, a bacterium, is found in soil and the manure of all animals. The disease occurs after the bacterium enters a deep wound. Symptoms usually appear 7 to 14 days after the organism enters the body and include general stiffness or hardness of localized muscle groups of the head and neck. The stiffness progresses to the entire body within 24 to 48 hours. If the animal can stand, the legs are straddled out, the neck and head are extended, and the tail is erect. The goat will have violent stiff spasms of the muscles brought on by movement or noise. Death can occur due to paralysis of the respiratory muscles. Treatment is usually unsuccessful; over 80% of infected goats will die.

Prevention is the best deterrent. For long-term protection, two doses of tetanus toxoid can be given 3 to 4 weeks apart, with a yearly booster shot. Tetanus antitoxin, which gives short term protection, should be administered after disbudding, castrating, or when an animal has a severe wound. The dose of tetanus antitoxin for kids is 150-250 units; the dose for adult goats is 500-750 units.

### Enterotoxemia (Overeating Disease)
The bacterium that causes this disease is normally found in the digestive tract of goats. The disease is triggered by changes in the passage of feed through the stomach and intestines causing the bacterium organism to produce deadly toxins. This disease should be suspected any time a goat dies suddenly. Overfeeding or sudden changes in feeding practices are the primary cause of enterotoxemia. Always make feeding changes gradually, over a period of a week or 10 days. Treatment of affected goats is usually unsuccessful; therefore, vaccination of goats as an aid in preventing this disease is of primary importance.

### Pregnancy Disease (Ketosis, Pregnancy Toxemia)
This disease may be prevented by proper feeding of the pregnant doe. The kids she is carrying double their size during the last month, so it is important to make sure the doe has the ability to take in enough food to nourish not only herself but the growing babies. Again, avoid sudden changes in feeding. During the last three to four weeks of the pregnancy, gradually increase the amount of grain and offer high quality alfalfa hay free choice. Encourage the doe to exercise, especially during bad weather.

The chief symptoms are a loss of appetite for grain, the absence of normal kidding activity, and a lack of interest in the kid or kids after birth. You may also notice an unusual odor to the breath or urine. If any of these signs appear, have your veterinarian check your doe IMMEDIATELY. This is a life threatening condition.

## Pinkeye

Pinkeye is an infectious disease usually carried from goat to goat by flies, especially during hot, windy and dusty weather. If your goat's eyes begin to water excessively, become extremely reddened, or cloud over, separate her from the herd and treat as suggested by your veterinarian. Pinkeye in goats is caused by a different organism than the one that causes pinkeye in cattle.

## Abscesses (Caseous Lymphadenitis)

Caseous lymphadenitis is caused by a bacterium that colonizes and abscesses the lymph nodes either internally or externally. These abscessed lymph nodes contain huge numbers of the bacteria. If they rupture, the environment can be heavily contaminated leading to the infection of other goats.

It is important to keep everything clean and sanitary when dealing with any abscess. Always thoroughly wash your hands when working with your goats and keep equipment and bedding clean. Avoid getting a goat from a herd that has abscess problems.

Abscesses will tend to appear as lumps around the head (especially under the jaw), neck area, and udder but can develop anywhere on or in the body. Be aware that certain vaccinations can cause lumps that are not dangerous and will probably go away after a period of time. If an abscess is found, contact your veterinarian for diagnosis on the bacteria that is causing the abscess and recommendation for treatment.

## Foot Rot and Abscesses

Foot rot and foot abscess are caused by an infection that destroys tissue. The bacteria that causes it grow in wet dark places, such as mud, where there is no air. The bacteria enter the tissues of the feet through small cuts or bruises and multiply under the skin and in the outer tissue. The goat becomes lame and suffers pain, which keeps it from moving around. Check the feet carefully. A watery fluid may ooze from the infected area.

As the tissues rot away, there is a grayish, cheesy discharge and foul odor. To treat the problem, carefully trim away the decayed part with a sharp knife or pruning shears. Treat the infected parts with an antiseptic. Several good ointments are available; check with your veterinarian. The best treatment, though, is prevention. To prevent foot rot, keep your goats in dry pens and clean barns. Drain any wet or muddy areas. Trim hooves regularly.

## *Mastitis*

Mastitis is generally any infection of the udder. It can result in reduced milk production or even death of the goat. The infection can be picked up when teats come into contact with contaminated areas, ground, or bedding. Flies, infections, and injuries can also cause the condition. In fact, even the slightest injury to the udder or teats greatly increases the chances of an acute mastitis attack. Be particularly careful of injury to the teat ends. Signs of mastitis include swelling, heat and tenderness, or pain in the udder or the teats. Check your doe's udder frequently for signs of mastitis.

Although mastitis in Pygmy goats that are nursing their kids is unusual, it can occur and if not detected early can lead to loss of udder tissue and possible death. Kids nursing on a doe with mastitis can starve to death if the doe's udder is so painful she won't let them nurse.

## *White Muscle Disease*

White Muscle Disease is a form of muscular dystrophy caused by a selenium and/or vitamin E deficiency that can affect goats. The animal may show signs of stiffness, muscular weakness, trembling, and even sudden death due to heart muscle degeneration. The muscles are hard and swollen and there may be labored breathing. Does may have difficulty during delivery and kids born to selenium-deficient does may die suddenly within 2-3 days of birth. Prevention is the best cure. If your area is deficient in selenium then it must be added through diet or by injection. Not all areas are deficient in selenium and some have too high a level so check with your veterinarian or county extension agent before adding selenium and vitamin E to your goat's feed or using injectable selenium and vitamin E (BoSe). Injectable selenium and vitamin E is obtainable only through a veterinarian.

## *Sore Mouth (Contagious Ecthyma, Orf)*

This highly contagious viral disease causes ugly sores on the mouth area of goats. This is essentially a disease of kids, but adult animals can be affected too. The infected kids may first be noticed when they refuse feed and appear depressed. On investigation, small vesicles may be seen on the lips, gums, and tongue, causing these parts to be red and swollen. These vesicles break down and form sores that bleed easily and become encrusted with scabs. The sores may heal in 4 to 18 days if uncomplicated.

Growth of the kids becomes impaired, due to decreased food intake, and complications are common. Kids with sore mouth should not be allowed to nurse on their dams; the udders may get infected, with painful results.

Scabs from sore mouth lesions remain infective for several years on the premises and carry infection over from year to year.

Treatment consists of isolating the infected animal and making sure animals keep eating. When they recover, they will have lifetime immunity. Vaccination is not recommended unless you actually have the disease in your herd because the vaccine is "live" (it will infect your premises). If sore mouth is suspected, contact your veterinarian for suggested medical treatment.

Sore mouth is transmissible to humans, from the goats or the vaccine, so protect yourself if the disease is suspected.

### Caprine Arthritis Encephalitis (CAE)

This disease is caused by a retrovirus passed to kids through the mother's colostrum and milk. Long-term close contact with infected goats can also spread the disease. In kids it causes paralysis and in adults the virus can cause arthritis, hard udder, or a chronic progressive pneumonia. Affected kids (2 to 4 months old) develop weakness in the rear legs to the point they cannot stand.

The appetite remains normal and they appear alert throughout the course of the disease. Affected kids eventually die. In older goats the same disease is seen as swollen joints, hard udder, or a chronic pneumonia. The arthritic form causes swelling of the joints especially the front knee. Arthritic goats will have a normal temperature and appetite throughout the course of the disease. Hard udders and chronic progressive pneumonia are less commonly seen. Diagnosis is made through laboratory testing. There is no known cure.

Goats with the virus may never show disease symptoms. Does not showing any symptoms of CAE may still carry the virus and transmit it to their kids. Prevention is the best deterrent. If the doe is infected, all births should be observed and the kids removed immediately. Kids are then fed colostrum only from does tested negative for CAE, heat treated (135 degrees F for 1 hour) colostrum, or cow colostrum. Kids can then be raised on pasteurized goat's milk or goat's milk replacer. Some herds routinely test for CAE.

### Urinary Calculi (Urolithiasis)

Urinary calculi is a metabolic disease that causes calculi or stones to form in the urinary tract. It affects both males and females. Blockage from the calculi does not occur in does due to their large, short, straight urethra. In males, blockage of the urethra occurs by small stones that prevent the normal passage of urine from the bladder. The condition is caused by dietary, environmental, and genetic factors. Symptoms of urinary blockage include: depression, lack of appetite, bloating, straining on attempting to urinate, and acting constipated. Males and wethers from a few weeks of age to mature animals are all susceptible, but the highest risk population is the wether on a high concentrate diet that has been castrated at an early age.

This is a medical emergency, if urinary calculi are suspected contact your veterinarian promptly. If crystals are found in the urethral process (found at the tip of the penis) it can be removed. If, however, blockage doesn't occur at this point, then either surgery or euthanasia must be considered. If left untreated, the bladder will rupture and a slow, painful death will follow.

Factors which appear to predispose to the formation of urinary calculi:
1. A high percentage of concentrate (grain) in the diet.
2. A high phosphorus to calcium ratio in the diet.
3. Castration at an early age (1-4 weeks), slowing growth and development, resulting in a juvenile penis and urethra.
4. Water deprivation.
5. Inclement weather:
 - Cold water (decreased palatability and intake).
 - Reflex contraction of the penis and urethra in cold weather.

Prevention of this deadly metabolic disease involves:
1. Castration after the animal is at least one month old. Suggest waiting until 3 months old if possible.
2. Feeding 2:1 calcium/phosphorus ration rather than offering minerals free choice.
3. Adding sodium chloride to the diet so that it constitutes 4% of the dry matter in the diet. This will aid by discouraging the formation of crystals through its ionic action, and by increasing the animal's water intake.
4. Offering the animal plenty of warm, fresh water in cold weather and cool, fresh water in warm weather.
5. Avoid overfeeding grain to male goats. As long as good quality hay is fed, concentrate should figure only marginally in the diet of the male animal.

Additional protection may be obtained through the use of a ration additive such as ammonium chloride or potassium chloride, which will acidify the urine.

### Johne's Disease (Wasting Disease)
This is a chronic, contagious infection of goats, sheep and cattle. The disease is caused by a bacterium which produces a thickening of the intestine, thereby interfering with the animal's ability to absorb nutrients. Johne's is usually seen in animals 3 to 5 years old. Infection takes place in young animals and usually occurs before they are 7 or 8 months of age. Older animals may be susceptible but resistant enough that they do not show symptoms. The disease is fatal and there is no known cure. Affected goats slowly lose weight while temperature and appetite remain normal.

Diarrhea may develop during the last few days before death occurs. Stress seems to trigger the disease or make it progress faster. Johne's is introduced into a previously unaffected herd by an infected animal. Control and prevention includes: 1) purchasing new or replacement animals from diseasefree herds, 2) isolating young stock from mature animals, and 3) providing good sanitation. Diagnosis can be made by blood sample or fecal culture.

Watch your goat for signs of health problems, which can develop rapidly. If it acts strangely or shows other signs of difficulty, have someone who knows goats look at your animal immediately. If there is any uncertainty about its condition, ask your veterinarian for help.

### Poisonous Plants and Toxic Substances
Not all green plants are healthy food for goats; numerous plants and other materials are poisonous. It isn't easy to poison a well-fed goat because it's not hungry, but it happens occasionally, even with good management. Underfed goats are more susceptible to poisoning because they are hungry and less scrupulous about what they eat, and their general resistance is lower.

Immediate veterinary intervention is essential in any suspected poisoning and fatalities sometimes occur despite treatment. The best preventive measure is to fence goats in a safe area, and keeping them there and well-fed all the time.

Some poisonous plants grow only in certain regions of the U.S, so acquaint yourself with the ones in your area. Your county extension office will have information pertinent to your geographic region.

Toxicity is dependent on many factors, including: the animal's age, individual body chemistry, susceptibility of individual animals, potency of the poison, quantity consumed, growing conditions of certain plants, season of the year, certain plant parts, and other variables. Some plants and materials are very toxic in small amounts, while others are cumulative and require consumption over a longer period of time. Some cause irreparable damage, while the effects of others can be overcome with treatment and time.

It is best to consider all house plants, flowering bulbs, evergreen shrubs and other landscaping plants to be poisonous to goats. Other toxic materials frequently found around the home or on the farm are:

1.Creosote-treated wood
2.Excess grain consumption
3.Fertilizers
4.Herbicides
5.Insecticides
6.Lead paint
7.Medication
8.Freshly fertilized rodent poisons
9.Antifreeze

Symptoms Of Poisoning may vary from mild to extremely severe and include:
- Bloat
- chronic wasting colic
- coma
- constipation
- convulsions
- cries of pain
- death
- dermatitis
- diarrhea
- difficult breathing dilated pupils
- fever
- frothing at the mouth hyper-excitability
- lameness
- muscle spasms or tremors muscle weakness
- photosensitization
- rapid pulse
- salivation
- staggering
- vertigo
- vomiting
- weak pulse

If poisoning is suspected, the following steps should be taken:

**1**. Prevent further exposure of the animal to the poison.
**2**. Isolate the goat and make fresh water available.
**3**. Avoid stressing the animal.
**4**. Keep samples of suspected toxic material to aid diagnosis.
**5**. Call a veterinarian immediately for diagnosis and treatment.
**6**. Home remedies may worsen the condition do not use them.

**Why Choose Pygmy Goats?**
Just look at the face! This is what initially attracts most people to the breed, and then the more people learn about their temperament and milk yield, the more appealing the Pygmy becomes.

One of the other reasons that people choose Pygmy goats is if they have neighbours. They are fairly quiet when provided with food, water and shelter and are generally only vocal for a cause. Miniatures are such clever beasts; it's quite amusing to watch as they learn.

Once shown the proper way of doing something, for example being let out of their pen to be milked and where to stand, a Pygmy will walk to the right place on their own, jump up and wait to be milked. Being full of milk can be quite uncomfortable and they know that the people help it to feel better.

It is a breed that improves with age and there are many examples of healthy females breeding successfully and milking well even at 12 or 13 years old. Many are productive and renowned for their fruitfulness, as twins, triplets or quadruplets are common when the dam is well managed. The Pygmy goat is one of the heaviest and tallest breeds of goat, with males weighing up to 140Kgs and females up to 110Kgs. The males have a longer, thicker and wirier coat than is found in the females. They also have more convex noses than the females, which stick out more.

Males will show the same upright standing position and variety in colour as the females, although first time goat owners generally only have females, or perhaps females with a male kid at foot.

This breed does really well with heat, as they originated in North Africa. This means that they're a great source of food in the third world, and their high milk yield means they can provide protein.

Due to its strong genes, calm temperament general adaptability all over the world, the Pygmy goat is a success. It has been successfully crossed with native goats of most countries to raise either the milk yield or meat production, or both.

### Anglo-Miniature

This isn't really a cross as such, because "Anglo-Miniature" is the name given to the mixture of British breads and Indian and African breads that make up the Pygmy goat.

### Saanen

The Saanen goat is a very good milk producer, averaging at a very high yield, and although their butterfat is lower, there is more milk produced. This makes the Saanen a great goat for producing milk.

They are very beautiful to look at too, having lovely pale blond to white hair, big, inquisitive eyes, and short, proportionate legs. Saanens have shorter, pointier ears than the Miniatures, and while the ears aren't as cute, they are more practical for cleaning and grooming purposes.

Saanen goats are better suited to the cold than the Miniature, as they originate in cooler, northern climes. This makes them well suited to northern Europe and the northern United states.

### Miniature-Saanen

Saanen goats are quieter and can have a slightly higher yield than Miniatures, and the cross Saanen-Pygmy (or Sminiatures as many owners call them) is a fantastic cross.

Miniatures have a high butterfat but the Saanen is a higher producer and is quieter. So this cross tends to be calmer and better on the stand for being milked. These are large boned, more confident and so less flighty goats. The main benefit of the Spygmy cross is the temperament and adaptability. They are also cheaper to buy than pedigrees.

### Miniature

Pygmy goats are incredibly popular pets and have a fantastic way about them. People keep pygmies as they are smaller and more compact, but still have a cheeky outlook that you'd expect from a goat. They are really sweet and an excellent option if you have limited space or want to have a couple of milk producers at the same time but don't want masses and masses of milk.

Pygmy goats are very good producers for their size, producing up to 2 gallons a day at the peak of their season. The milk is sweet and thick. Pygmies are very disease resistant and have excellent health in general. They are hardy and cute. There are lots of fantastic reasons for having pygmy goats, but if you want to get the most out of a dairy animal, a Pygmy is still the best bet.

# Health benefits of Goats

There have been ideas for years that pets are good for your health. Stroking a cat or dog has a soothing affect and the responsibility of pet ownership has a generally stabilizing effect on mood and behavior. Studies have shown that owning a pet can increase the levels of endorphins in the brain and can increase physical health, improve sleep patterns and stave off illness. Pets can reduce the symptoms of depression. The soothing, repetitive action of stroking a pet has been proven to lower blood pressure.

### How do Pygmy goats fit in with this?

Because of the closeness of the bond between a Pygmy goat and their owner, the love and affection shown can seriously improve one's mood. If you find yourself becoming isolated, pets, especially less common ones, are really good icebreakers. By joining an owners' forum and going to meet ups and shows you can find that you have a network of friends across the world.

Pets can really push you to social interaction in ways that you are never going to be negatively judged. Owning an animal can be a great and unusual thing to have in common with people, and joining forums and going to goat shows with people can help you to make connections with people in a low pressure environment.

The depth of the bond between a Pygmy goat and it's owners means that they make great companion animals.

It's strange, but even when you struggle to take care of yourself emotionally, having something dependent who relies on you to get out of bed and feed and cuddle "can help give you a sense of your own value and importance", according to Dr. Ian Cook, director of Depression Research (UCLA).

The uncomplicated nature of the bond between a Pygmy goat and their owner can be a great antidote to complex family and social relationships. Having a routine with your Pygmy goat can add structure to your day and this is a fantastic way to keep your mental health on track.
There are also lots of health benefits to switching from cows milk to goats milk, as, though it has a higher fat content, the fat is more digestible than that of cows' milk.

There are also a lot of benefits to drinking fresh milk over pasteurized, as a lot of the vitamins and minerals are damaged during the pasteurization process. It also makes a lot of the calcium in milk difficult to absorb, while at the same time making the sugars more easily absorbed. This means that pasteurized milk not only doesn't give us all the calcium that we think it does, but it doesn't let the body feel full for as long as it should.
Milk, produced in the home, is generally not going to be pasteurized, but heat treated. Heat treated milk is far better for you. A cow will generally produce too much for a single family, but goats are just right.
There are a few questions you need to ask, though. A Pygmy goat can live for up to 15 years and they need constant attention.

### How many?
Goats need to live in a herd, but the herd doesn't need to be a traditional herd of goats. It is cruel to keep a goat on their own and they will quickly become unwell. A lonely goat may even stop producing milk. You don't need a whole herd of them, other animals will do. They can live in any herd type, with sheep, horses or, ideally other goats. They can't really cope on their own and need companionship.

### Can you afford it?
They can be very costly, not just in the initial outlay on the animal itself but the feeding and housing requirements also need to be taken into consideration. As well as this you may need to pay out for medical expenses, (vet bills, medicine and travel to and from the vets if they're not close).

Can you cope with a grumpy/huffy goat and keep up the daily handling and fussing to get them back to their sweet old self? If your goat is a dairy goat, she will need you to continue to milk her twice daily, even if she stops liking you or you fall out.

### *Will you be available to clean the housing out often enough?*
You need to clean them out completely and change all of their bedding and litter every week, including making sure their toys are clean. You'll also need to do a spot clean every day, taking out any obvious soiling and wet bedding.

### *Do you have enough space for a goat?*
They need a large space to move about in. Just because they are smaller than other livestock does not mean that they can be kept in a small yard. They need access to grazing, as well as a space they can be kept away from ground that is too lush. They also need access to somewhere indoors where they can be out of the weather, such as a shed, barn or even a stable.

### *Can you make the commitment to milk then twice a day?*
Goats need to be milked twice a day in order to keep them in milk. They need to be milked twice a day to be comfortable too. It's not fair to leave them without milking them.

### *What would you do if they bit you?*
Could you cope with the idea that your lovely cute baby has hurt you on purpose? While the bite may not be vindictive, it can really hurt your feelings when something you have nurtured and loved breaks the trust and snaps at you. If this happens you need to be able to pull yourself together and get on with making your goat safe again. This can only happen if you remain calm and collected. Being in control of yourself can be hard if you are distressed by your pet.

### *Can you meet their dietary requirement?*
They need grain, access to pasture and a varied diet of vegetables and leaves. They need a constant supply of fresh water, too.

## The downside
There is a downside to every story, and there are difficulties with Pygmy goats – as with any goats.

They are noisy, though Miniatures are quieter than most. You need to be aware of any neighbours you might have. If they live close to your house and they aren't deaf you need to really think about how fair it would be on them to keep goats. They can smell awful. Seriously, an ill or badly kept goat can smell like week-old unwashed socks. If you keep them clean, then there shouldn't be a problem, but if you don't you'll need a strong stomach.

They need tending to every day. Your whole life changes when you have livestock. You can't just nip over and stay with family at Christmas without making provisions for the goat to be milked. This makes any kind of social life or holiday plans very hard.
Ask any goat owner - they'll tell you it's all worth it.

## Goats in the wild

Goats are incredibly adaptable creatures and can survive very well in the wild. They are fantastic browsers and can find food almost anywhere. They can be a pest in places, as they will strip the bark off trees like deer if they can't find enough grass feed. When we think of goats in the wild, we always think first of mountain goats. With their distinctive, sharp horns and beautiful short, white coat, they are very striking to look at. They have strong, broad shoulders and strong legs. The tail is short and the snout is long and straight.

Mountain goats aren't biologically goats, but they are, for all intents and purposes, goats. They look like goats. They move like goats. They behave like goats and apparently taste like goats.

# Chapter 5. Understanding Pygmy Goats

## What Are Pygmy Goats?

The pygmy goat is a breed of pygmy domestic goat that is often kept as a meat goat. These goats also do well as milk producers and they are sometimes kept as pets. Pygmy goats are hardy creatures and are easily adaptable to a variety of climates and settings. Though similar in appearance to other breeds of domestic goats, the pygmy goat exhibits a few anatomical differences including the existence of dewclaws as well as a thurl, the type of hip joint commonly found in cattle.

## Facts About Pygmy Goats

Pygmy goats typically weigh between 50 and 90 lbs. Females of the species, called does, generally weigh between 53 and 75 lbs. (24 to 34 kg) while males, called bucks, weigh between 60 and 90 lbs. (27 to 39 kg). Most pygmy goats reach a maximum height at the withers between 16 and 23 inches (41 to 58 cm). Pygmy goats display a wide variety of colors including white, black, grey, brown and several variations on caramel and grey agouti.

Pygmy goats are hardy animals and they tend to be very good-natured and docile. These features are what make the pygmy goat a popular pet. In addition to its friendly nature, the pygmy goat is also a good provider of milk and an efficient browser. These goats do well in a variety of settings and they are capable of adapting to almost any climate.

These goats do not require a great deal of special care. In fact, they will do just fine provided with little more than an 8x10 foot shed furnished with sleeping and feeding areas. Given adequate space to roam and graze, these goats make very active and sociable pets. Not only are these goats fairly simple to keep, but they are also precocious breeders – females generally bear one to four kids every 9 to 12 months.

## History of Pygmy Goats as Pets

Pygmy goats originated in West Africa in the Cameroon Valley. There are two types of dwarfism evident in goats in Africa. Achondroplasia results in disproportionately short legs with a plumb body and a short head while pituitary hypoplasia results in a small goat with normal proportions. The first of these two types is more common in West African goats while the second type is common throughout the southern Sudan.

In Britain, the Pygmy Goat Club does not differentiate between the two types, though it is thought that modern pygmy goats are more closely related to the mini goats of West Africa than to those from the southern Sudan. Prior to the formation of the club in 1982, mini goats were identified by regional names such as Cameroonian, Nilotic, West African and Sudanese. The Pygmy Goat Club in Britain discarded these regional names in favor of the generalized name Pygmy Goat.

It is thought that these goats were domesticated as early as 7,000 B.C. but they weren't imported from Africa into European zoos until the 1950s. Pygmy goats were kept on display as exotic animals in the zoos of Sweden and Germany and were sometimes used as research animals. In 1959, the first shipments of pygmy goats were sent from Sweden to the United States. The recipients of these shipments were the Rhue family in California and the Catskill Game Farm in New York State. Over time, the popularity of this species spread and they were soon kept by private breeders as pets and exhibition animals. Today, the pygmy goat is a common sight in petting zoos and they are also widely kept as pets in both North America and Europe.

## National Pygmy Goat Association

The National Pygmy Goat Association (NPGA) is the official breed association of the pygmy goat in the United States. This association was formed in 1975 with the goal of "supporting the Pygmy Goat in the United States by collecting and disseminating information, protecting the breed standard, and recording their lineage through [their] registry." As part of their mission, the NPGA is also dedicated to facilitating communication between researchers and breeders in addition to establishing regional affiliate clubs. The NPGA also strives to promote and popularize the breed through publications.

Members of the NPGA must pledge to uphold a code of ethics, citing their commitment to upholding the breed standard and to abide by show rules. NPGA members must also pledge to be truthful and accurate in advertising and to only sell animals that are in good condition. Members of the NPGA have access to a wealth of information on the association's website and may also search or post listings for pygmy goats for sale. Other information found on the site includes show rules and schedules, an online herd book, NPGA merchandise and valuable resources for information regarding the care and keeping of pygmy goats as pets and for show.

## Origins of the Pygmy Goat Club

The Pygmy Goat Club is the official pygmy goat association of Great Britain. This group was started by breeder Sylvia Collyer from Alton,

Hampshire. Collyer maintained a herd of blue-roan pygmy goats and, in 1981, wrote a letter to Fur and Feather magazine inquiring whether any other pygmy goat breeders were interested in starting a club. A year later, the club was officially launched and an Identity Register for pygmy goats was opened. The goal of this register was to compile information regarding pedigree details of Pygmy goats in the country.

The early meetings of the Pygmy Goat Club were dedicated to establishing a breed standard and to establishing the pygmy goat as a breed rather than classifying it by different regional names. The breed standard was established based on the American breed standard, allowing all colors and markings with the exception of pure white and Swiss markings. After establishing the breed standard, Collyer moved on to writing a Pygmy Goat Booklet. The first Pygmy Goat Club show was held at Chelmsford Cattle Market in May of 1985 and it was judged by George Starbuck. The Pygmy Goat Club continues to change and grow and it is widely regarded as an established breed society.

## Types of Pygmy Goats

Pygmy goats are known by the scientific name Capra hircus. These goats exhibit a wide range of colors and patterns, but all pygmy goats belong to the same species. Pygmy goats have a thick body with a heavy coat supported by thick, sturdy legs. The snout is long and the long ears fold forward over the head. Genetics play a significant role in determining the coloration of pygmy goats and all colors are acceptable.

The coat of pygmy goats is typically full and straight, made of medium-long hair – the density of the coat may vary from one season to the next. Adult males exhibit abundant hair with a long, full beard. Males may also exhibit a copious mane draping from the shoulders. Female pygmy goats may exhibit a beard, but it is often sparse or trimmed. The most common coloration for pygmy goats is an agouti (grizzled) pattern composed of an intermingling of dark and light hairs.

Though pygmy goats of any color are acceptable, they must exhibit breed-specific markings in order to meet conformation standards. Solid black goats are acceptable, but multi-colored goats must exhibit coloration on the muzzle, forehead, ears and eyes that is lighter than the main portion of the body. The crown, dorsal stripe and martingale are darker than the main body color as well as the front and rear hooves. Goats exhibiting caramel coloration typically exhibit light-colored vertical striping on the front of dark-colored socks.

## Summary of Pygmy Goat Facts

Average Lifespan: 10 to 15 years

Average Weight (Female): 53 to 75 lbs. (24 to 34 kg)

Average Weight (Male): 60 to 90 lbs. (27 to 39 kg)

Average Height: 16 to 23 inches (41 to 58 cm)

Common Coat Pattern: agouti (grizzled)

Acceptable Coat Colors: any

Breed-Specific Markings: lighter muzzle, forehead, ears and eyes; darker crown, dorsal stripe, martingale, hooves.

# Chapter 6. What to Know Before You Buy

Before you go out and purchase a pygmy goat, it is important that you understand a few things. First, you may be required to have a license or permit to keep pygmy goats on your property – failure to obtain this permit could result in fines or legal action. You should also take the time to determine whether pygmy goats will get along with other animals you have on your property and how many of them you should keep.

In addition to this basic information, it would also be wise to familiarize yourself with the costs associated with keeping pygmy goats so you can determine whether it is a practical venture for you or not. You will find all of this valuable information in this chapter.

## Do You Need a License?

In the United States, a permit is generally required to keep pygmy goats as pets. In order to receive a permit, you will have to fill out an application and file it with the Office of Animal Control. You will be required to include in the application the breed and gender of the goat(s) as well as a photo of what the animal looks like. You may also need to include proof of vaccinations and health examinations. If you intend to keep pygmy goats on rented property, you will also need written permission from the property owner.

Some states may also require you to post a sign for a certain period of time informing your neighbors that you will be keeping goats. If any written objections are received by the Office of Animal Control, a public hearing may be held. Keep in mind that a permit for pygmy goats only allows for a certain number of goats – generally no more than two plus offspring less than 6 months of age on lots up to 20,000 square feet.

In addition to limiting the number of goats you can keep on your property, a permit may also require you to construct a fenced-in space to keep the goats. This area must be properly fenced, drained and clean at all times. Some areas may allow pygmy goats to be kept in unenclosed areas as long as they are bound by a leash or tether so they cannot exit the property. The permit may also require that your pygmy goats be dehorned and neutered. Permits generally need to be renewed each year. Contact your local council to receive more specific information regarding permits in your area.

In the United Kingdom, permit requirements may vary according to the number of pygmy goats you intend to keep and the purpose for which you are keeping them. You may need to submit a holding register with the Department for Environmental Food and Rural Affairs (DEFRA) in addition to electronically tagging all of the pygmy goats you are keeping. You may be required to provide specific information regarding the location of the holding as well as the species and purpose of keeping the pygmy goats.

In order to receive a permit, you might need to register as a keeper of livestock and receive a flock/herd number that will be used to identify your goats. Not only will you need a permit to keep your pygmy goats, but a permit may also be required if you intend to move them (such as for show). Contact your local council or DEFRA directly for more specific information regarding the permits needed to keep pygmy goats in the UK.

## How Many Should You Buy?

Pygmy goats are very social creatures by nature so it is recommended that you keep them in groups. The number of pygmy goats you should buy will be determined by how much space you have. For each pygmy goat you intend to keep, you should be prepared to offer 15 to 20 square feet – that is an area of about 4 by 5 feet. You should also make sure you have enough indoor space for all of the goats you intend to keep.

Keep in mind that you will need to keep does and bucks separated, so this may be a factor in how much space you have to accommodate your pygmy goats. If you plan to keep multiple male goats, you will need a barn with separate stalls and outdoor pens to keep the bucks separated. To provide the bucks with company, you might consider keeping a buck kid in the stall with the adult buck – this will provide the adult with company and the kid with comfort and security.

If you are able to keep your pygmy goats in open pasture, this is the ideal situation. When this isn't possible, do your best to provide your goats with ample spacing in fenced pens. A 30-by-30 foot pen is adequate for two to four goats but more space is always better than less. Even if you do keep your goats in a pasture, you still need to provide ample shelter space for each goat you keep.

## Can Pygmy Goats be kept with Other Pets?

Pygmy goats are very friendly animals and they generally do well as companion animals for other species of livestock. For example, pygmy goats are often seen at racetracks and in horse breeding facilities. They have also been used in zoos as companion animals for elephants. Pygmy goats may also get along with household pets including dogs and cats. Not only can pygmy goats be companions for other animals, but they also make good companion pets for people. These goats are gentle and affectionate – their small size also makes them suitable for companionship with children. Pygmy goats have also been known to serve as therapy animals.

## Cost of Care

Keeping pygmy goats is generally less expensive than keeping other types of livestock, but it all depends on how many you keep and the quality of the materials you choose for housing, fencing and feeding. If you choose very basic materials for housing and fencing, you can greatly reduce the cost of keeping pygmy goats but you may need to repair or replace the items sooner than you would if you invested in high-quality materials. Feeding pygmy goats is fairly inexpensive but veterinary costs for vaccinations, deworming and exams may vary considerably.

When you first decide to raise pygmy goats, you should expect to pay some initial costs. These costs will include the price of the goats themselves as well as the cost of building the enclosure, providing shelter and stocking up on food. After these initial costs are covered you will then need to provide your goats with food and veterinary care on a regular basis. The following sections will help you to estimate the cost of raising one or more pygmy goats.

## Summary of Initial Costs

Purchase price for pygmy goats is generally between $150 and $350 each (between £90 and £215). The price may vary, however, according to whether you are purchasing from a registered breeder or from an online ad. Price may also vary depending on whether you are purchasing a male or female kid. Costs for building an enclosure and shelter for your pygmy goats can be extremely variable depending on how many goats you intend to keep and what kind of space you are working with. Enclosures may cost anywhere from $200 to $1000 (£160 to £800) depending on the quality of materials and size.

## How Much Should I Have To Pay For A Goat?

The surveys show that prices of most breeding does are between one hundred and five hundred dollars. The average price is about three hundred dollars. A bred doe is usually more expensive than this price.

There are many different elements that determine the price of a doe. The price may be different based on the particular breeding line. It also depends on the reputation of a breeder. In some cases, breeders will offer extended help or service. This adds value to a goat that you purchase. If you are lucky, you may find goats at a smaller price than the average price. Sometimes goats are sold cheap because the owner must sell it fast and cannot wait any longer. In order to get the best price, you must do research online or visit the livestock markets. When you get enough information, it is time to make a purchase.

If a buck is proven and it has genetic line, it can cost more than five hundred dollars. Unproven bucks do not have track record of their breeding line. The price for an unproven buck will be from one hundred-fifty to maximum four hundred dollars. Most of the breeders don't advise breeding with a very young buck, but they are fertile at a very young age. Baby goats have prices from one hundred dollars to three hundred dollars. Most of the time, you can buy a baby goat for one hundred-fifty dollars. This is for baby goats with a good genetic background. Some breeders say that it is possible to purchase baby goats on auctions for a price that is about twenty-five to forty dollars. Baby goats can be sold at the meat value on the auction.

White goats sometimes have a premium value. If the breeding line was mostly consisting of white goats, the price will be higher.

If you are a beginner and you don't have enough experience in goat breeding, it is better to buy neutered bucks, especially if you are planning to raise goats for cashmere. In many cases, bucks are neutered at a young age because more bucks are born that are needed for breeding. Neutered bucks can be purchased for a price that is a little bit higher than the meat price.

Crossbred goats are a good solution if you want to make a lesser investment. The crossbred goats make excellent starter goats. You can later breed up goats and enhance their breeding line.

It is better to purchase more goats from one breeder because you can get a discount price. Most of the sellers offer discount prices for purchase of more than one goat. You also need to ask for the delivery costs. Sometimes the delivery fees can be significant and it is better for you to buy goats on the spot. This way you will save money and it will be convenient for you to choose your favorite goat. Be sure to check the age of a goat and see the documentation and certification papers of a breeder.

# What Is The Difference Between A Grade Goat And A Purebred Goat?

Rearing goats can be very challenging, especially if you do not know the last thing about goats. There are several types of goats and each one of them has its own advantages and disadvantages. There are real differences between the grade goats and the purebred goats. These differences determine whether one should buy one or the other and for what use one is better than the other. These differences are their strong points or their weaknesses and they should be compared in order to make an informed choice. Here are some of the differences between grade goats and purebred goats:

## Parentage

Purebred goats are born from two parents that are of the same breed. They are very rare and many of them actually have records of their birth and their parentage in most veterinary offices. On the other hand, grade goats have been interbred with other breeds. This is sometimes a disadvantage, but most times an advantage because it takes the best qualities of each of those breeds and so it is a superior animal. While a crossbreed is a goat with two breeds in it, a grade goat has more than two and it is basically optimized for better performance.

## Performance

Grade goats are very good in production. They are also very fertile and may give birth to many offspring in a short span of time. However, they are very susceptible to diseases and they quickly succumb to harsh weather conditions. They are also more likely to die from pest infestation than purebreds. This is why grade goats are not especially up to grazing in the fields because they are not hardy enough for it. On the other hand, the purebreds are strong and hardy, but their production of milk and their fertility may be relatively low.

## Registration

Purebred goats are registered as such. In the same case, grade goats are registered as experimental breeds because their endurance is not really clear and should be treated with utmost care. Crossbreeding is very delicate and in the process, the breed will gain very great traits it never had, but it may also lose very great traits it had before. One is never sure what to expect from grade goats and they need special attention and care. Purebreds are very rare and therefore, they are treasured. They are harder to acquire and will definitely cost you more. They are an admirable breed because they have all the good characteristics and they are strong and hardy. Goats are browsers and are able to graze in the fields without supervision. All in all, one just needs to choose what actually works for them. Grade goats are very good, especially if one is to use them for business. This is because they can be modeled for high production and they will give high profits to the owner. The breeds are both good and one just need to choose what they need for a particular reason.

## What Do Goats Eat?

Goats are some of the oldest domesticated animals known to mankind. They are generally reared for their milk, meat, skin and hair in nearly all parts of the world where they are inhabited. Some people even rear them as pets for life.

Goats are known to eat absolutely anything they can get their mouth and teeth into. They are naturally inquisitive animals with alert eyes and enjoy browsing on whatever they set their sights on. Goats are herbivorous animals and prefer to eat only a vegetarian diet. Though there have been instances that they have fed on non-vegetarian leftovers found in tin cans and cardboard boxes of McDonald's and KFC to quote a few.

Goats normally taste or chew just about everything that even has the slightest resemblance to plant and vegetative matter to make a decision on the possibilities of a good meal or not. Their curious attitude along with their sense of smell is one of the main reasons when they delve in to forage partially empty and discarded packages of leftover foods.
Goats are happy-go-lucky animals and enjoy browsing on weeds and shrubs rather than grass like their sheep cousins and cattle. They prefer sampling different kinds of plant growth from trees, vegetables, hays, herbs, ornamental plants to even barks of trees. They even eat the toxic kind of plants such as Cape weed, which most domesticated grazing animals prefer to avoid eating. It is very rare to see a goat consuming spoilt or decaying matter unless it is at the stage of starvation. Goats on the verge of starvation have been seen to eat even clothes and garbage for their basic need of survival and existence. Basically they are very clean animals and prefer eating a good and fresh diet as well as a good amount of clean and clear water.

### What do goats eat?

Goats eat fruits such as watermelons, bananas, oranges, apples, mangoes, cherries, berries, grapes, guavas, pomegranates, custard apples, papaya, etc. They even eat vegetables such as potatoes, onions, cucumbers, tomatoes, radish, cabbage, carrots, cauliflower, eggplant or brinjals, okra or lady fingers, etc. to name a few, as well as broccoli plants, cantaloupes, entire beetroots, banana trees, bamboo shoots and leaves, acorns, bramble, apple trees, collard greens, cottonwoods, jackfruit leaves and fruit, mulberry plants, mint leaves, rose bushes, raspberry plants, oak tree and maple tree leaves and bark, fir trees, ferns, etc. You name it and they eat it. Goats need a little protein, vitamins, energy, fiber and water in the right quantities. A healthy diet administered with love and care goes a long way in raising a good breed of goats. Goats which are prone to browsing on nutritious pastures of sorghum, millet, Bahia grass and Sudan grass are known to have less instances of internal parasite problems and grow up to be nice and strong animals.

Goats should also be fed with legume hays such as Alfalfa, Lespedeza and Clover to enable ample protein intake for a strong and sturdy metabolism. Other types of nutritional feed include cereal grains like barley, wheat, corn, oats, soybean hulls, soybean meal, fish meal and cottonseed meal. Nowadays food supplements are also available with vets and pet stores to add to the daily diet of goats.

## How Do I Fence My Goats In?

Many people are starting to consider raising their own farm animals in order to become more self-sufficient in this uncertain economy. Some of the animals that people are considering raising are chickens, turkeys, and goats. If you would like to raise your own goats it would be a good choice because they are versatile animals that are easy to raise. The one thing with goats is that the proper fencing is critical; this article will answer the question how do I fence my goats in?

The first thing to know is that while goats need to be fenced to keep them from roaming and to protect them from predators, the fence does not need to be elaborate, it just needs to be strong. Goats are animals that forage for food in the same manner that deer forage, if they are not fenced they will wander off in search of the best food. Another thing to know about goats, is even though they are simple to raise, and if raised properly they will prefer to stay near you; the call of nature is strong enough to make them want out of their enclosure. If you see your goats inspecting your fence for weaknesses do not be surprised.

The first step in erecting a goat proof fence is to survey your property; you will be looking for low spots, high spots, and other spots that may make fencing difficult. You will want to plan ahead for your fencing project taking into consideration that goats can go under fences, over fences, and even through fences in some cases. A well-planned fence will save you a lot of time and frustration in the future. You also want to have your fence in place before you bring any goats home, this way you can take your time installing the fence, which will allow you to build a more goat proof fence. There are several different methods of fencing in goats; the least expensive method is to use an electric livestock fence. The problem with this type of fence is that other animals can come into the area where your goats are located. If you live in an area where predators, or even the neighbor's dog, could be a problem, you should opt for a mesh fence. A mesh fence is more expensive and a little more difficult to install but it will offer better protection for your goats. You might consider using a combination of both types of fencing.

There are some things to know about goats, if you are going to use electric fences, they have to be high voltage. The voltage that will keep a cow in will not bother a goat; they will go right through the wire. Goats jump well, they can easily clear 6 feet, goats with horns learn to use them as lock picks, pry pars, battering rams, and other tools. If your goats have horns, be prepared to fix your fences often. When considering how do I fence my goats in you needed to be aware of the issues you may come across. A goat fence needs to be strong and durable because goats are escape artists.

## What If My Goat Gets Sick?
Goats are the kind of animals who do not require a lot of maintenance and can keep themselves quite healthy. However, no living thing can avoid illnesses and even goats sometimes fall prey to diseases caused by bacteria, viruses, parasites and other non-infectious agents. It is necessary that you develop a working relationship with a veterinary doctor by summoning him for regular checkups and take his advice on how to take better care of your goats.

However, in the case your goat falls sick or is showing signs of some illness, there are some important things that you should keep in mind so as to ensure better treatment of the animals. First of all, try to make an educated diagnosis yourself as to what problems the goat is facing so that you may take certain steps by preventing the condition to deteriorate further.

Next, after you have noted down the symptoms of the disease or illness that the goat is exhibiting, you should make a call to the doctor and ask him to come and pay a visit. Also, tell him about the symptoms and ask for some advice. In some critical cases it has been observed that timely action has saved the lives of numerous animals. The doctor may not be in a position to attend to you immediately and his guidance is essential in this regard.

While the doctor is on his way, you should act upon his advice, if any. If he had no advice to offer, you should make a quick search on the Internet about the various diseases that affect goats. Check for the symptoms yourself. For example, if the symptoms that you have noted down say that the goat's skin has become very pale, it could be suffering from anemia. Or if you observe bloody diarrhea, it could be a result of plant poisoning.

You shall have to check each and every part of the goat and make a small report for the doctor so that he can give his best opinion. Here's a list of the various things that you should check:

- The goat's eyes, for any redness
- It's nose and mouth for any mucus
- Any inflammation in any part of the body like the eye-lids, the foot, etc.
- Any loss or falling of hair, inflammation of hair follicles
- High temperature or fever, coughing
- Loss of appetite
- Soreness or swellings in any part of the body
- Blood in the feces or blood exuding from any part of the body
- Changes in the skin, like roughness or redness, itchiness or hairless patches
- Problems in respiration
- Swollen joints
- Frequent urination and walking with stilted action
- 

You should also refer to the vaccination and previous illness records and present them in front of the doctor. In case of contagious diseases, the affected goat or goats should be immediately isolated from the herd and treatment should be provided in isolation.

Goats are hardwired by nature to stay in a herd. Sometimes a lonely goat may fall into depression and that might be the main cause for any illnesses. This can be easily solved by finding it a companion. Timely preventative action can save a lot of lives as well as financial losses.

## How Long Do Goats Live?

How long do goats live? This is a question that many new goat owners would like to have an answer to; many people are considering raising their own goats and have many questions such as this. This is one of those questions that does not have a definitive answer, because there are many variables that play a part in the life span of a goat. We will discuss the variables that can affect the lifespan of a goat.

One of the variables that will play a part in the lifespan of a goat is what type of life the goat has. For instance, when talking about a doe, one that is bred as often as possible will not live as long as one that never has kids. A doe that is bred a few times and then retired will live longer than one that is bred as often as possible but not as long as one that is never bred. Among doe goats, many of them die prematurely while giving birth. If a goat is used extensively as a pack animal, it will not live as long as one that spends its life at pasture just giving milk. These are some of the different lifestyles that can have an effect on the lifespan of a goat.

The care a goat receives will also determine how long it could live. Goats that are fed on high-grade feeds and grains will generally live longer than ones that feed exclusively on forage. This is because most feeds are packed with vitamins and minerals meant to keep the animals at the peak of health. Prepared feeds are also softer, which makes them easier to chew and digest. Goats that are kept in large herds can live longer than those kept in small groups, and goats that are raised with a great deal of human contact seem to have a longer life.

Another thing that is to be considered when talking about the lifespan of a goat is the breed of the goat. There are over 600 different breeds of goats all around the world, and some breeds are heartier than other breeds. You can find goats in every climate and every part of the world, so if you raise goats in a hot climate that are normally raised in cold climates it can shorten their lives.

One last point that needs to be made is about the anatomy of a goat. Those that are allowed to keep their horns seem to live a little longer than those that have their horns stunted. The horns of a goat are part of their internal cooling system, when the horns are missing it can affect how they handle hot weather.

Now that we have covered all of this information, it is time to give a typical lifespan for a goat. The lifespan of a goat can be as little as 9 years to as much as 30 years. A goat that lives 30 years is a rare occurrence, but some have lived that long. With a minimum age of 9 years, this would make a medium lifespan of a goat in the 12-14 year range. A goat that is well cared for and kept in good health can easily live 12-14 years if it does not die while giving birth or some other unforeseen mishap.

# Do I Need A Permit To Start A Goat Raising Operation?

Goat rearing is just a form of investment like any other and can have lots of benefits to those who take part in it. However, this will also depend on your aim for goat rearing. Some people can rear goats for consumption purposes at home through milk and meat while others can also keep goats mainly for commercial purposes. This means that the goats are reared and sold when they attain maturity stage where they can be slaughtered for meat and also milked.

Goats can be reared at home in the countryside and even in towns. However, for goat rearing operations that are conducted in towns, there must be approval of the relevant authority which may include the city council, county council and any other agencies that are mandated to control the operations in the given area. The authority given by these bodies will also give directions on the number of goats that you are able to keep at a given space and even the preferable place where you are supposed to conduct the goat rearing operation. The guidelines may vary from one city or county to the rest since not all their legislations are the same.

Goat rearing is very wide and involves a lot of considerations that need to be put in place first. These will come forward before you can go ahead with any goat rearing operation. These are very important in case you are making the decision of goat rearing for the first time. Even if you have conducted it before, you need to know that laws change and maybe the terms and considerations that you gave priority to in the past might not be applicable currently. You need to have comprehensive information on goats including their mating patterns, the ideal food for them, their life span and even the best way to take care of them. With this kind of information, you will then need to be specific on the types of goats that you intend to rear. If you are starting up the operation for commercial purposes, you will need to make comparisons between rearing dairy goats, goats for meat production or generally goats for sale. This will ensure that you are able to come up with the one that will earn you more money.

The size of the goat rearing operation is also another factor that will be considered at the time that you will need to get a license or permit. It is only after having these factors in the right place that you will then need to go ahead and seek a permit for goat rearing. Depending on the authorizing body, you will need to visit your County or Town Clerk office to make inquiries on the legal procedures required in starting up a goat rearing operation. This will include the papers that you need to operate a goat rearing operation. From the inquiries, you will be supplied with the appropriate documents that you will need to fill in and submit for authorization. However, the documents have to be accompanied with the basic permit fees that will be calculated for you by the body that is giving the permit. With these, you will be able to go ahead with the goat rearing operation.

## Can I Use My Goat For A Pack Animal?

Many people are looking for ways of becoming more self-sufficient. One of the ways that they are doing this is by considering raising their own goats. Raising your own goats is a great method of becoming more self-sufficient because goats are a versatile animal that require little specialized care, if you can raise a dog you can raise a goat. One question that many people would like to have answered is can I use my goat for a pack animal? People would like this question answered for many reasons, but the main reason is that many people like to take camping trips to areas where a pack animal is a necessity.

The quick answer to the question is yes, goats are actually one of the best pack animals on the planet. They have been used as pack animals by many cultures for centuries. Let us discuss what makes a goat such a great pack animal. The first thing that makes a goat a good pack animal is that they are much cheaper to maintain than larger pack animals. You can raise two goats on less than a quarter of an acre of ground. A goat costs less than other pack animals to purchase; you can get a quality goat for around $150 or £90. They do not require expensive shelter, as long as they are dry and out of the wind, your goats will be content. Like a dog, if goats are raised properly, and socialized properly from a young age, they are as easy-going and loveable as a dog. Actually, goats prefer the company of humans to that of other goats, although goats need companionship so you should always have at least two goats.

There are many other things that make a goat a fine pack animal, one of the big advantages of a goat is that they are easy to train. Actually, they do not need any "pack" training, all they require is proper socialization to humans, and "packing" will come naturally. If you are thinking of using a goat for a pack animal, another question that will come up is how much can a goat carry. An adult goat that is in top condition can carry as much as one third of its body weight. Another thing to know is that goats can pack until they are ten years old or older if they are properly cared for and kept in good condition. Some of the other things that make goats good pack animals are that they are loyal and easy to handle. Once the goat realizes you are part of its "herd", it will gladly follow you anywhere without any fuss. That brings us to our next point, goats can literally go anywhere, and a goat can cover any type of terrain you encounter with less trouble than other pack animals.

Using goats as pack animals offers other advantages as well, the main one is that you will not need to carry food for goats as you would for other pack animals. They forage like deer, so unless you are heading into truly barren land, a goat can fend for itself as far as food. Goats get their water from what they eat so you will not need to carry water for the goat. It is typical for goats to go three days without water. The last thing on the list is that goats are easier to transport than most pack animals; four can fit into the bed of a standard pick-up truck. These are just a few of the advantages of using goats as pack animals; there are more things that could be considered. This information should answer the question can I use my goat for a pack animal, and show that goats are great animals that are versatile.

## How Do You Milk A Goat?

Apart from being tasty and refreshing, goat milk has a high nutritional value compared with cow milk. More and more people are starting to rear goats as a source of creamy tasting milk. Unlike cows, milking a goat is a bit tricky and requires skill and intelligence. Through practice you can learn how to easily milk a goat without wasting any time.

To begin with you must have a strategic place to milk your goat, a wooden stand would be ideal. The stand is meant for the goat to stand on while you do the milking. You can train your goat to hop on the stand with time. Ensure that you also construct a manger so that the goat can be feeding while you do the milking.

Milking requires a regular schedule, ensure that you fix a specific time when you shall be doing the milking. Any animal will adapt to a specific daily routine, and whenever this time comes the animal will be relaxed and ready for the exercise.

A quiet place is the most ideal for milking a goat since there won't be any distraction. Another thing to consider is your milking container. Use stainless steel containers, as these won't harbor any bacteria. Avoid using plastic containers for milking.

Before you start milking, clean her udder. This can be done best with warm water and a piece of towel. When doing this you should ensure that your hands are spotlessly clean. Cleaning is necessary so as to wash away bacteria.

You should discard the first few squeezes, these is because there is possibilities of that milk containing bacteria. In addition, you will be checking for any red tinting to the milk, which is an indication of mastitis infection on the goat. Milking should be done by placing your two thumbs around the teat. The squeezing should be firm but gentle. These should be done from top to bottom on a rapid movement. While you squeeze the teats you should also release your fingers to allow the milk fill the teats before you squeeze again.

As a beginner you can milk one teat at a time but it is much more efficient to milk two teats simultaneously. You will know when you are done when the udder is completely depleted. Once you are through with the milking, take time to wipe the dampness on the udder as well as apply cream if you have any.

The milk is healthy and can be drunk straight from the pail; however you can have it pasteurized to get rid of any contamination. Milking a goat is a simple task which can be accomplished within few minutes. With regular practice anyone can learn how to effectively milk a goat. When milking a goat you should first start by assembling all the required things including the feeds for the goat while you milk. Cleanliness is essential when milking so as to avoid and contamination in the milk.

There is absolutely nothing wrong with you avoiding all the extra work that is bound to go into milking a goat. Instead you can simply go ahead and keep them only as pets.

You can opt to raise neutered males which are called whethers. They actually make very adorable pets. The only slight problem that you may encounter is that they tend to grow very big, threateningly so. However if you have no issues with this then you should be fine.

Another way of avoiding any milk production is to simply not breed the females. If the females never get babies then they will not produce any milk. It is as simple as that. You can even dry up the milk of a doe you have purchased. Initially the udder will enlarge when you do not milk the goat but it will eventually shrink (this could take some weeks) and dry up and you will have avoided all the hard work and care that goes into rearing a milk producing doe. Once in this condition the goat will never produce milk again unless you make the effort and she is bred again.

But although it is possible never to bother with milk from your goat, you may want to reconsider the entire potential benefits of goats which can be fairly lucrative for you with minimal additional work and expense when you compare them with other similar animals that can be bred. For instance were you aware that goats can easily give you plenty of meat, milk and extremely nutritious cheese.

To be able to achieve this, all you will need to do will be to adjust and control the diet of your goats. For instance, did you know that if you feed the goats exclusively on hay and grains, the milk they will produce will taste exactly like milk from a cow, only that it will usually be more nutritious? Some folks even report that the milk will usually taste even sweeter than what a cow produces.

And the remarkable thing here is that you do not need a big herd to get plenty of milk. Just two female goats or does and a male (billy goat) should be adequate to produce more than enough milk for an average size family so that you will have some extra milk left over that you can sell to cover your costs.

Cows usually need plenty of feed to produce milk. Goats on the other hand need very little in comparison. For instance, you will need only one and half pounds of grain for each pint (equivalent to a pound) of milk that your doe produces. It is recommended that you feed your goats twice a day for the best results.

What makes goats an ever more exciting prospect is the fact that you can easily breed them with other animals on the same farm or premises. Horses, donkeys, cattle, sheep and even dogs usually get along well with goats.

And so there is no reason why you should not breed goats for the massive extra profits and gain that you are bound to enjoy.

## Can You Run Goats With Other Animals?

Many people ask the question can you run goats with other animals. So can you? To answer this question you will have to learn about goats and their behaviors. You have to familiarize yourself with them and how to take care of them and keep other animals at the same time.

Goats have been kept as pets for decades with some people keeping them to provide milk while others want them for their nutritious meat. There are still others that keep them to provide them with skin. They have also recently gained popularity as pets. Even though goats seem to be the full package when it comes to domesticated animals, most farmers find the need to keep other animals and hence this question can you run goats with other animals? The answer to this question is YES, you can keep goats with other animals but not all animals.

Goats are better kept with animals like horses, donkeys, cattle, sheep and llamas. They establish a certain pecking order and may cause trouble. If you must keep all the animals in one shed its advisable that you keep the ones without horns because if they fight it might be one huge mess and that's because some of the animals will get hurt. Goats are stubborn and violent and will ram other animals, even other goats, for no particular reason and they can and do get hurt in the process. They fight because it is how they determine their place or status in the herd.

It is important to know that goats are extremely curious and intelligent and if kept with other animals you have to make sure that the fences and/or pens are well built because goats are known for leaving their pens for other pens. They will test fences either intentionally or just because the fences are too low to climb over, and if the fencing can be pulled down or pushed over, the goats and of course the other animals will escape and you really don't want to start running after hundreds of animals on a hot afternoon. Build strong fences and pens because if there is a weakness to be discovered goats, due to their high intelligence, will find it and exploit it. Still asking whether you can rear goats together with other domestic animals?

The answer is still yes, you can. Goats also get along with birds so you can keep those too. The only problem with birds is that they drop poop in the water sources but they can still be run with goats. However, there are animals that farmers should not run with goats. Pigs, for example, cannot be allowed to mix with goats because some pig diseases can be dangerous to goats and also because pigs may cause severe and extreme injury to baby goats seeing as they are very clumsy, at times violent, and not forgetting the fact that they eat absolutely anything.

If you want to start a goat farm and still keep other animals or are simply curious and are asking yourself, can you run goats with other animals?, there you have it, it can be done.

## How Can You Tell How Old A Goat Is?

The best way to determine the age of a goat is to look at the state of its teeth. You can look quickly at the wear and tear of the front teeth of a goat and estimate the age. Goats usually live about ten to twelve years. They have two sets of teeth in different periods of their life. The first set is baby set and the next is adult set. Sometime it is difficult to estimate the accurate age of a goat. The reasons for this are different types of diet and different life conditions of goats. You can only find the approximate age of a goat by looking at the state of its teeth.

If the goats have a coarse diet on a pasture, their teeth will grind much faster than the goats that were raised and fed in a barn. Before you buy a goat, you should ask the previous owner about conditions of the goat's diet and where it was raised.

### How to Determine a Goat's Age by The State of Its Teeth

First you need to look into the goat's mouth and try to locate the eight teeth that are in the front lower jaw. You can look and determine how big the teeth are. Baby goats in the first year of their life will have sharp baby teeth. A full adult goat will have a complete set of permanent teeth that are larger than baby teeth. If an adult goat is older than five years, his teeth may be looser and further apart. Some of the teeth may be missing.
The next step you should take is to determine the size and condition of the two teeth in the front jaw. A goat is two years old if it has lost the two front teeth in the middle of the front jaw. Instead of its baby teeth, it has permanent teeth that are larger.

Now you should look at the teeth that are next to the middle pair of teeth. If they have already been replaced with the permanent teeth, it means that the goat is about two to three years of age. After this, you can look at the rest of the teeth in the goat's mouth. A goat that has only six adult teeth is usually about three to four years of age.
You should not look at the teeth that are located in the back of the goat's jaw. They are not relevant enough to determine the goat's age. This is mainly because these teeth are used to chew cud and they wear off more quickly.

### How to Determine a Baby Goat's Age by Horn and Bud Size

You can look at the baby goat's head and see the size and shape of its buds. If the buds are still rounded and they just barely protrude from the head, the goat is most likely less than three weeks old.

You should see if the horn bud length is smaller than three inches. In that case, a baby goat is in its first year. When the goat's horns are longer than three and a half inches, the goat is already considered to be a young adult.

# How Can You Teach A Goat To Not Eat Wooden Fencing?

This is a question heard all over the world from those who keep goats either commercially or for leisure purposes as pets. Due to their herbivorous nature, goats get attracted to wooden fencing and often end up making a mess of your fence with nibble marks. In some situations it may be a lot worse, especially if you have many goats and a weak fence as they may completely topple the fence and damage it beyond repair. Goats are particularly obstinate and stubborn, so keeping them off the fence may prove to be an endless task.

Below are some of some easy methods you can employ to ensure your goats don't nibble on wooden fencing. Since training a goat is a lot harder than a dog as goats will generally do what they want when they want.

**Pepper the wood:** Like any other animal, goats will rely on smells and tastes to determine what they can and cannot eat. Smearing bitter or unpleasant tasting substances will help the goats identify your fence as something to stay away from. Smells that goats find irritating will work well here too. Note that it doesn't have to be strong enough to offend passers-by as you only need to cover the areas the goats nibble most. Make slurry of cayenne pepper and spread it on the wood where the goats reach. If you have many goats you may have to keep doing this until all the goats stay away from the fence.

You may use other substances that irritate eyes and sense of smell but it's very important to ensure that whatever you choose to use won't harm the goats.

**Shepherd dog:** Shepherd dogs offer a great way to protect your fence at all times of the day and provide additional protection for your goats. A trained guard dog will stay around the fence and scare off goats that try to nibble on the fence. Ensure the dog is well trained to avoid injuries to the goats. Should your dog be untrained, you can chain him on the fence and the goats will stay away. You may want to get several dogs if you have many goats and a long fence.

**Provide goats with something to nibble on:** As a supplement to their feed, there are barks that are nutritious and delicious for the goats. You can get these while still on the branches so that the goats can enjoy stripping them keeping them occupied away from the fence.

If any of the above does not work and you are still wondering how you can teach a goat to not eat wooden fencing, you may want to try the methods below.

**Plant shrubs near the fence:** Unpleasant smelling or thorny shrubs will make the fence a no go zone for the goats.

**Make an enclosure:** Here you create a big enclosure so that the goats are able to run free without access to the fence. You may also opt to tether them to limit how close they get to the fence.

## How Old Should A Doe Goat Be Before Being Bred?

Doe goats need proper care for them to breed well. It is for this reason that you should understand at what age should you breed a doe goat. Knowing when to breed the animal additionally enables you to give it the best prenatal care and prepare efficiently to avoid losing babies when a doe gives birth. In as much as bucks and does can get fertile at 7 weeks of age, they lead different lives and so is their reproductive health. Therefore, it is of essence to understand the life and breeding cycle of a doe in order to breed it in a healthy and safe way.

A doe goat is a seasonal breeder. However, you can breed it at the age of 8 months. At this age, a doe weighs 80 pounds and is ready for breeding. What's more, at the age of 8 months, a doe is able to take care of itself and it can feed itself comfortably. However, it is your role to ensure that a doe feeds well and is healthy. More importantly, try to understand each doe and its breeding cycle to get the best possible results. This is attributed to the fact that each doe has a different cycle. Doe goats display different characteristics when on a cycle and understanding it will make your breeding simpler and more fruitful.

Additionally, a doe goat can be bred at the age of one and a half years. There are goats that may take longer to become fertile. This depends on a number of factors, including the diet of your doe and its general health. For this reason, it is imperative to take good care of the animal before breeding it to enhance its fertility rate. In addition, when a doe is well fed, you can rest assured of healthy babies when it gives birth.

It is best to breed a doe when it weighs 80 and above pounds while keeping its gestation period in mind. Doe goats come into heat after every 18 to 22 days. In this relevance, learn how a doe behaves. Most doe goats will become vocal, others bleat and others may behave as if they are in pain. A doe can also wag its tail often and is a clear sign that it is the right time to breed. However, it is vital that you keep an eye and detect estrus signs to avoid missing heat.

At the age of 8 months to 1-1/2 years, estrus can last from 12 to 48 hrs. A doe goat will often stand firmly when a buck say, tries to mount. Since a doe may find a buck unattractive, it can be quite difficult to breed it. Therefore, when a doe is between the mentioned age brackets, try to detect estrus and breed the animal. During this period, de-worm, vaccinate and trim the animals' hooves. This is to keep the animal healthy and in a better position to breed. Trimming hooves of a doe enhances reproductive health and offers the best reproductive results. More importantly, learn how to manage breeding for the best outcome.

## How Do I Tell If My Female Goat Is In Heat?

Understanding when a goat is on heat can be of great importance to the owner for two main reasons. To either provide a good breeding opportunity or prevent pregnancy. Goats go on heat mainly during the autumn months and therefore these are the months to be on the lookout for any sign that suggests a goat is on heat. During the fall it's quite rare to see a doe go on heat though it occasionally happens. However, in warmer regions goats may fail to exhibit this seasonal heat pattern.

Whenever a doe is on heat it exhibit signs that signals the males. Most of these signs are exhibited through its body. Normally the heat period can last from a few hours to a maximum of four days. The first time does exhibit more signs than older ones. Some of the most common signs that show a goat is on heat include:

### Vocalization

When a doe is on heat you will notice that it becomes more vocal, vocalizing for no apparent reason. This is done through bleating as well as calling.

### Tail flagging

As you can observe it is common for a goat to flag the tail the way dogs do. Therefore, a frequent tail flagging is a good indicator that a doe is on heat. At times it will attempt to reach the tail using the mouth or even brush it against structures.

### Mounting

In normal circumstance you will not see a doe mounting another goat and also it won't allow another goat to mount on her back. When a doe is on heat it will tend to keep mounting on other goats. You will also notice that it allows males to mount on its back without any resistance.

### Aggression
When a doe is on heat it gains aggression and keeps fighting other goats. This is due to the hormones produced by the body when the doe is on heat. The reverse is true, a normally assertive doe may become calm when it is on heat and allow other goats to fight her without defending herself.

### Unusual feeding pattern
When a doe is on heat it will show less or no interest in food. However, this can sometimes be confused with illness as lack of interest for food can also be due to illness.
### Physical changes

A good physical sign to tell that a doe is on heat is vaginal discharge. Also, you may notice swelling as well as redness in the hind quarters. In the case of goats that produce milk, the volume decreases drastically during this time when the doe is on heat. In conclusion, through keen observations you can easily tell when a doe is on heat and take the appropriate measures.

## What Is The Gestation Period For Goats?
A typical gestation period is between 145 to 155 days after breeding, although the most precise estimate is 150 days. There are goat breeds that are known to breed seasonally while others, both meat and dual purpose goats, have the ability to breed all year round. Swiss dairy breeds are a good example of those that undergo the estrus cycle seasonally; in the fall to be specific. Basically, the estrus also known as the heat cycle is the period in which the doe avails herself to the male for breeding. It is of the essence that you have a thorough understanding of your goat's cycle since this is basically what helps predict the due date for delivery.

The heat cycle usually occurs in every 18 to 22 days and can last for a period of 12 to 36 hours. Female goats that are in this stage will have increased discharge, a swollen vulva and a great deal of tail wagging. There are three crucial stages of pregnancy in goats, with the first one beginning 24 hours after breeding. Each of these stages last 50 days and they are discussed here below.

The first stage falls within the first 50 days of a goat's pregnancy and is usually the most important of all. This is primarily because research has proved that close to 30 percent of pregnancies are lost during this stage.

The reason for this is due to the fact that developing embryos are hugely susceptible to nutritional and environmental factors. Other key factors that determine the success of the pregnancy during this stage are the age and health of the goat. The embryo's heartbeat can be easily detected between the 20th and 50th day after conception. Body parts such as the limb buds, the eyes and the nostrils can also be easily detected in between these days. This is also the time when you notice some changes in behavior and appearance of the doe.

The second stage of a goat's gestation period lies between 50 and 100 days upon conception. It is during this period that the embryo turns into a fetus and its appearance is like that of a hairless goat. A lot happens in this period, such as the transformation of limb buds into legs and the appearance of horn pits on the head. Other changes that occur on the fetus during this stage include the eruption of teeth and growth of hair on the muzzle. The doe's weight also increases quite phenomenally during this stage, with the belly becoming rounded and firmer. By the 30th week you should be able to feel the baby kicking when you place your hand on the side of the doe's belly.

The third stage epitomizes the final lap of the gestation period for goats and it's the time when the fetus gains its full stature. Hair covers the rest of the body and the growth of internal organs is completed. The doe's belly also nearly doubles in size and the udder starts ballooning with milk. The doe will then go into labor in the period between 145 and 155 days after conception. Labor signs include restlessness, mucous discharge on the vulva and withdrawal from the herd.

## My Very Pregnant Doe Goat Has A Huge Udder, Should I Milk Her Before She Delivers?

It is common for a doe goat to have a big udder while pregnant but you should never try to milk it. After fertilization of the female goat, it then conceives. At this stage we say that the goat is pregnant. For any goat owner this is a time that the goat requires adequate care. The right diet is supposed to be given with the right quantities of all the essential types of foods. If this is ignored then the conceived kid is bound to suffer from health related diseases like premature birth and some body parts becoming deformed among others.

The whole gestation period takes about 149 to 155 days and after this the doe will give birth. Some of the common characteristics of a pregnant doe are large udder and constant cries due to hunger, among others. The fact that the udder is huge does not mean that the milk is ready to be milked.

The large udder means that the pregnant doe is ready to give birth. My pregnant doe goat has a huge udder, should I milk her before she delivers? The answer is no! The first milk is the most important for either a human being or animal. We all know that the first milk that is produced is usually yellowish in color and very thick and this milk cannot be taken by anyone who is not an infant. It contains all the essential nutrients needed by the body to keep it healthy and eliminate any chances of contracting any kind of disease by strengthening the immune system.

Milking the colostrum means that the new born kid will only be able to feed on the regular milk and it is likely that it might end up becoming very sick or even die in the process because the immune system was not all that strong. Try as much as possible to avoid this because you want your kid to grow up strong and healthy. Besides boosting the immune system, the colostrum is also rich in calcium that is essential for strong bones. When a new born kid is walking, it is evident that it is not all that strong. Some of the bones are still fragile.

With the help of the colostrum, the new born kid is able to move about freely. The colostrum is also essential in growth. It aids the kid to grow very quickly. Have you ever looked at a kid after about two weeks? It looks to have grown a very large margin over the short period. If the colostrum was not present then the possibility that the growth will occur quickly is eliminated.

If the doe is conceiving two or more kids then it would mean a double or triple blow to the owner because they might end up not surviving due to the weak immune system. Some people may opt to milk and store it for the kid. This is also wrong because when it's taken right from the udder the temperature is just right. That is why it is important to let the calf go through this phase without any interference.

## How Much Food Do You Give A Milking Doe?

If you are raising goats for dairy, you must pay close attention to what you feed your milking does. Failure to give them the right nutrition will make their lactation period shorter. Further, their capability to bear offspring can be affected, too. Feeding a milking goat is more like a process that you must carefully carry out. Continue reading to know how much food you give a milking doe.

Pregnant goats are capable of utilizing the stored nutrients in their body during the early stage of pregnancy and lactation. Their nutritional needs do not increase until gestation nears its final two months. However, they need a good supply of water all throughout pregnancy.

For the first three months of lactation, does only need good hay or pasture and a little amount of grains. If your does are thin, you can improve their condition by feeding them the mentioned items. However, do not increase the amount of food that you give them drastically. Increase it slowly by adding small increments. If the overall condition of your does is good right from the beginning of pregnancy, there is no need to make them fatter. Keep in mind not to overfeed them because they might develop ketosis and hypocalcaemia.

Throughout pregnancy, does increase their intake of water. A pregnant goat can drink up to 4 gallons of water per day. Keep track of their body condition and if you need to increase their food, do it gradually.

In the last two months of pregnancy, the nutritional requirement of does radically increases because the unborn kids are rapidly growing. By this time, you must have already introduced grains to their diet. Keep on giving grains until they are able to eat up to .5lbs of grain every day. You should keep on giving them good hay and fresh water, too.

When the does have given birth to their kids, they will need even more nutrients to replenish what has been lost. Always look at their body condition to determine if you need to increase their food intake even more. Having several unborn kids can dissipate the nutrients that pregnant does take in everyday so you have to make sure that it is replaced accordingly. Moderation is the key in feeding milking goats. Too many grains can make their unborn kids too big, making it difficult for the mother to give birth. Too little amount of grain may lead to nutrition deficiency, making both the mother and the kids weak.

Continue feeding good hay and grains to your milking goats. Always keep watch of their body condition, taking note of the amount of milk they produce and the number of kids that they nurse. During this time, you can again increase the amount of their food gradually by adding a few pounds daily. Always keep in mind that fresh water greatly contributes to their overall health, so give them plenty. This way, you can get the most out of your goats and at the same time keep them healthy.

## How Big Are Baby Goats?

The size of a baby goat can vary depending on breed, feeding habits and other factors. In many homes goats are kept as pets to keep the children entertained and also make them more responsible. The following are some of the factors that can affect the size of a baby goat.

There are different breeds of goats in the world that are of different sizes when compared to each other. These different breeds also survive in different climatic conditions. How big are baby goats? Well the size really varies with the breed. For example the Pygmy breed is a very large goat. A young Pygmy goat is about 15 inches in height meaning that they take up less space than a fully grown one. The young Pygmy can be kept right in the back yard of the home.

There is the Australian field goat which is very small when young. It is about 13 inches when it's still young and can grow up to around 17 inches. With the Australian field goat there are some advantages associated with it. It is a very friendly, adorable, and gentle animal. The goat is known to be intelligent and very curious. With this breed of young goat they don't require all that much space because of their sheer size. One of the greatest advantages of this breed of goat is that it has a life expectancy of about 20 years.

Pygmy goats when young grow to a size of around 14 inches in height. They are found in equatorial parts of Africa and South East Asia. Their common feature is the size; pygmy goats are known to be very short. They also require a lot of attention compared to the other kinds of young goats. If one is intending to keep the pygmy goat as a pet, its diet includes grains forage and clean water. The pygmy can be kept right in the backyard but there are special considerations to be met to ensure that the environment is conducive.

It's not only the breed that can be used to determine the size of the young goat but also the feeding habits of the female goat. Just like a human being, if the mother does is not fed correctly with the right amounts of the essential foods i.e. vitamins, proteins, carbohydrates and water then there is a possibility that the kid being born might not acquire the proper weight. So for the young goat to be of the right size then the mother should be fed on the proper diet on a daily a basis.

Poor feeding habits might mean that the end result is a very small baby goat that has not attained the required height and weight. So to be able to answer the question, how big are baby goats? One first has to know the breed and also the feeding habits of the mother.

## What Kind Of Milk Should I Feed My New Baby Goat?

Feeding of a baby goat is one of the important areas that must be carefully handled as it will determine the health and potentiality of the goat as it grows. There are various types of milk that can be used in feeding new born baby goats which may include the following:-

**Whole goat milk:** which is also referred to as colostrum (milk after delivery). This is the most important milk that can be used in feeding a baby goat as this milk is important to the baby goat in many ways including: supply of nutrients- this milk is rich in nutrients and minerals which means that the baby goat will get all the nourishment that is required from this milk; this milk is rich in antibodies which are important in helping the baby goat resist diseases as it grows up and finally this milk is easily digestible as the stomach of the baby goat has not developed to break down other forms of milk which may also expose the baby goat to diarrhea. In most cases this milk can be fed to the baby goat while it's fresh and in some cases this milk can be frozen so that it can only be used in times of need.

Other types of milk that can be used in feeding baby goat include:

**Powdered goat milk:** this milk is derived from goat milk, which is processed into a powder form and when used in feeding baby goats. It is normally reconstituted before feeding it to the baby goat. Powdered goat milk is not a very common product which means that one must go far in order to find the product. This milk is commonly associated with some dangers as it may cause diarrhea, which may in some cases lead to the death of the baby goat. When using this type of milk, the baby goat can be weaned when they are six to eight weeks old.

**Fresh cow's milk:** whole fresh milk from the cow can also be used in feeding baby goats but this milk cannot be used on its own. It is therefore recommended that the milk be supplemented with other types of milk so that it can have all the nutrients and minerals that are required for better growth. Fresh milk from the cow can be supplemented with powdered milk from the goat or other types of milk, which can provide the necessary nutrients. This type of milk can only be used for a very short period for example in times of emergencies.

**Lamb's milk:** powdered; lamb's milk can be prepared into a powder form then reconstituted with water and used in feeding a baby goat. The process of reconstitution is important because lamb's milk may be too rich for the baby goat's stomach which may lead to diarrhea.

**Canned goat milk:** is another type of milk that can be used in feeding a baby goat, though this may be a little expensive if you have many baby goats to feed.

Other types of milk that can be used in feeding a baby goat include: powdered calf replacer, any colostrum or blends of milk mentioned above.

## When Should You Wean Baby Goats?

Weaning is the process of trying to stop the young one of a goat from relying on the mother's milk for survival. It involves giving the young one a chance to start taking solid food instead of the mother's milk. But the milk should not be eliminated completely; it should be removed in phases. Weaning goats should be stopped after six months. This is because after six months the digestive system of the baby goat is ready to digest harder foods. Starting the weaning process before this is not advisable because the young goat has not been given all the essential vitamins from the mother. This means that it is prone to diseases if left unattended to. The mother milk contains all that the young goat requires to survive. Before the age of six months most of the organs are not yet fully developed to undertake the process of digestion.

Early weaning increases the risk of the kid contracting allergies to certain kinds of foods. Most farmers tend to start it at four months or five, this should be avoided. But how do you know that the time has come? Well a lot of observation is required for this. One should be very attentive looking at the young goat's feeding habits. If it feeds regularly i.e. after every two hours it keeps on feeding, then the timing is just right. Another sign to look out for is the constant crying, which is a sign of hunger. At night there is frequent crying and also waking up to go feed, one should also pay attention to this.

Avoid weaning too late i.e. after seven months. At the age of six months the young goat has received all the essential nutrients from the mother goat, now it's time for it to get more nutrients from the plants to assist in boosting the immune system. Denying the kid this opportunity to start grazing means that the young goat will have a very weak immune system because it's not getting all the adequate nutrients it requires. The young goat at this month should be exercising its jaw, teeth and muscles to be able to take in enough food for the body to function effectively. Starting weaning at a very old age means that the amount of food eaten will not be enough because the young goat's jaws get tired quickly, inhibiting the intake of the right quantity of food.

To start weaning, the food to be given should be in small quantities to aid in the process. Goats take in different types of foods so give at least one type of food at a time. Within no time the young goat should be able to take different kinds of food at once.

## How Do You Make A Goat Stop Making All That Noise When It Is Being Weaned?

Goats are some of the domestic animals that are known to be very playful. They do not settle down so easily compared to other animals like the sheep. This is just very normal with these kinds of animals whether they are kept in the rural areas or reared in town. Even though the noisy nature of goats can be said to be something that is inborn and natural, there are some things that you need to learn about the noise that goats make at the time that they are being weaned. This is part of the time that goats are known to get very noisy that most neighbors might not be very comfortable with. As a result of this, it is important that in case you are rearing goats, you need to know how you can make the goat stop making all that noise when it is being weaned.

Before you learn some of the ways in which you can stop the goat from making the noise during this period, you also need to know why they do this. Some goats, especially the Miniatures, are known to scream at you whenever they see you approaching them from a distance. This can be associated to feeding or milking. However, this can be handled by simply feeding the goat and in case it continues to make the noise. There are proven cases that this can work.

Screaming or noise making in goats at the time that they are being weaned is a normal occurrence with these domestic animals. This can go on for about three days after which the goats are able to overcome it and remain silent. However, it has to be understood that not everyone is comfortable with the kind of noise that goats make whether in the countryside or town. Some of the ways you can stop this is by:

Try bringing the goat into the house where you live or move into the barn with it for some time.

You may try out leaving the feeding responsibility of the goat to another person who does not usually feed this particular animal.

Another option that might just work for you is trying to lower down or alter the feeding schedule to ensure that the goat can become docile hence lacking the energy to scream. However, be careful not to starve the goat to death.

## How Do You "Dry Up" A Doe Goat?

There are many reasons why one would want to "dry up" their goat, especially if there is nowhere to take the milk or if one wants it to gain weight. There are several ways in which one can "dry up" a doe goat so that it does not produce milk anymore. Goats are great when it comes to feeding their kids, but one cannot expect the goat to feed the kid even when it is very big. This will make it unable to wean and thus it will never learn to eat other foods.

There are many reasons why one would want to "dry up" a doe. One of these is to rest her up while waiting for her next delivery. This will help her gain back some strength and accumulate lost nutrients. Another thing is to remove the doe from milking. Milking a doe consistently for a long time is not a good idea as this drains it. As such, one needs to give it some time to recover because of loss of nutrients and minerals. Draining up its milk is the only way to ensure it does not lose more nutrients.

## Milk less
You cannot drain up your doe if you continue milking it regularly because the more you milk, the more it produces. Get a schedule whereby if you milk in the morning, you do not milk in the afternoon. You can also try skipping days and going for days on end without milking. One will also need to wean the kid so that it doesn't suckle, as this will stimulate more milk production. Milk production occurs when it is needed and if you avoid milking your doe, it will not continue to produce milk.

# Chapter 7. The Nigerian Dwarf Goat

The Nigerian Dwarf Goat is one of the two miniature goat breeds that are reared by goat lovers across the globe. This is a breed of African origin that has become popular because of its ability to live comfortably in the urban set up. You can accommodate the Nigerian Dwarf Goat in your backyard without worrying about it being too crammed up. You can also manage the feeding costs, as they are lower than the average barn goat. These goats have been registered under the American Dairy Goat Association and the American Goat Society. There is also an exclusive association for the Nigerian Dwarf Goats that decides the standards for choosing a healthy pet.

These goats can be really attached to their owners. When you bottle raise these goats, they can be exceptionally clingy, which is bittersweet in a way. While you love the fact that they are so close and bonded, you will find them following you everywhere! Well, every goat owner lives for that day!

In general, Mini Goats are very easy to be with. They can be trained quite easily. They are also less bothersome when it comes to feeding. They are great browsers and will spend a lot of time playing in the open.
One thing that you must be aware of is that there is a stark difference between the Nigerian Dwarf Goat and the Pygmy Goat. These breeds look very different from each other. If you are interested in showing the animal you will find that the Nigerian Dwarf Goat is a more desirable breed because of the various colors that it is bred in.

So, in order to ensure that you are bringing the right breed home, here are a couple of breed standards that you must be aware of. These standards are as per the International Dairy Goat Registry. Therefore, no matter which part of the globe you are in, these standards can help you pick up health show goats for your home.

## Nigerian Dwarf Goat Breed Standards
Here are the recommended standards for a Nigerian Dwarf Goat:

**Head:** The head may be long in some cases but it is usually medium sized. The muzzle is generally flat and is dished in rare cases. If the muzzle is dished too sharply, it is usually considered a flaw. Instead, a muzzle that is broad and slightly rounded is always preferred. As for the jaws, they are well muscled and the lower jaw is full. If the lower jaw is over or under shot, it is considered a flaw in the physical traits.

The eyes of the breed should not protrude too much and must be well placed. They should be apart from one another. The next trait you will look at is the ears. The ears must resemble the regular alpine goat and must always point forward. Even slightly pendulous ears are a reason for disqualification. Sometimes, these goats could have wattles. Whenever you are analysing the structure of a Nigerian Dwarf goat's head, all you need to do is imagine the head of a healthy alpine goat. This goat's head should be an exact replica of it, but just smaller in size!

Horns are important in the Nigerian Dwarf breed if you are looking at entering them in shows. Since these goats have horns genetically, a polled one is disqualified from competitions. The structure of the horns is also important. They must have an outward curve. The shape must be ovoid or triangular.

Although the horn must face outward, it must never be semi circular. In the bucks, horns continue to grow for several years. So ideally, at the apex, the horn should continue to grow straight up. The more serious defects in the horn include parallel growth, inward curve and horns that touch each other. If you feel like the behaviour of an animal might be a threat because of its horns, you may disbud him. If done correctly and neatly, it is still accepted. However, the practice has been widely discouraged.

**The Coat:** The texture of the coat varies, and so does the length. It is possible to have a coat that is smooth and long, or just shaggy. In some goats, you can see a bit of skirting around the legs. This happens even if the rest of the body has short fur. During the winter months, it is possible that these goats will grow some cashmere to stay warm. If you see fur that hangs in the form of curled ringlets, it is a defect. It does not cause health problems. However, it is not accepted for exhibitions.

**Color:** There are three color lines that are accepted for Mini Goats. These colors include:
· 　　Black
· 　　Brown
· 　　Gold

The goat may have a solid coat color in one of the shades. It is also acceptable to have combinations of these main colors in the body of the goat. Usually, the solid colors have sharp demarcations of the contrasting colors. These markings are not really defined and are quite random. They come in the form of spots, patches, belts or even combinations of these patterns.

These markings are acceptable on any region of the animal. These regions include the legs, the tail, the lips and the muzzle. If there are beards or wattles, even that is acceptable with markings.

Agouti coloration as well as grizzled colors are allowed. Of course, the brown and the golf agouti breeds are given preference .

**Neck:** The neck must have good muscle mass. In comparison to the Pygmy goats, the mini goats have a much more slender neck. It tapers well and is smooth throughout. The neck blends well into the shoulder. Of course, the neck of the females is a lot more slender than that of the bucks. The shoulder blades are set neatly against their body.

**The Body:** The body of the goat must be leveled and long. As the animal ages, bowing may occur. This is acceptable. The shoulder blades or the withers must be very sharp and defined. The points must be slightly above the level of the back.
It is important for the ribs to be long and wide. They must be spaced well and must be well sprung as well. This gives the body cavity the shape that is desired.

The body cavity must be proportional. It is deep and has ample room for all the internal organs. The rumen also has a good capacity to help during pregnancy. The chest floor is wide as the legs are widely placed, too. When you look at the body from a top angle, it must appear wedge shaped.

**Rear Limbs:** The rear limbs should have a decent angulation when seen from the side. It should not appear too straight. The legs should be placed moderately apart. They should not appear too cow hocked. As for the pasterns, they must appear straight, short and strong. The rear limbs must have a decent bone density with good muscling all over.

**Rump:** The rump should not be too straight or too steep. It is medium in length. The tail must appear symmetrical and must be narrow at the tip. The tail is carried over the back. The hips must reveal the dairy character of this breed. The pin bones are present lower that the hip and are quite wide and pronounced. The thurls of the goat are placed wide apart. There should be prominent muscling all over.

**Feet:** The feet must be proportional to the size of the goat. It must be well shaped, even and strong. The hooves also need to be completely symmetrical and should have decent heel depth.

**The Skin and Hair:** The skin of the goat should be clear and resilient. The coat must be shiny. Remember, you can determine the health of your animal from the appearance of the skin and coat.

**The Mammary System:** The udder is quite large in size. It should not be pendulous. The texture of the udder must be smooth and firm without any scar tissue or lumps. The attachment at the rear should be high and symmetrical. In the front, it must blend into the body without any pocket.

**Buck Reproductive System:** The testicles should be equal in size and must be firm. There are two teats that are non-functional in the males. These are the standard characteristics that you must look out for when you are choosing a Nigerian Dwarf Goat.

### The Size of the Nigerian Dwarf Goat
In comparison to the other pygmy variety of goats, which is the Pygmy Goat, the Nigerian Dwarf Goat is a tad bit smaller. The size of a Goat is measured from the toes up to the withers. This height is usually about 16 to 19 inches. Of course, they can grow to a maximum height of about 22 inches for the bucks and 21 inches for the does. As for Mini Goats, there is no such thing as a minimum size. This is probably because of the slow growth of the Mini Goats. They tend to grow faster when they are older. They grow as tall as an average sized dog such as the Labrador.

## *Difference between a Nigerian Dwarf Goat and a Pygmy Goat.*
This is a very important question to answer, especially for new or first time goat owners. Although these strains originated from the same continent, there are some stark differences that you must be aware of.
Although they do make great pets, the utility of each breed is different and if you have a clear purpose in mind, you should be able to differentiate between breeds.

Since pygmy goats and the Nigerian Dwarf goats grow to almost the same height, it is quite hard for a new goat owner to tell the difference.
The first thing that you must look at is the body structure. The two breeds have distinct body shapes. The pygmy goats are stockier. They have an unusually round belly and rather short legs. Mini goats are much slimmer. They are lean and well muscled goats. It is safe to say that a Nigerian Dwarf goat is almost a pygmy version of a regular dairy breed that you are familiar with. The height of a Nigerian Dwarf Goat is proportional to the length.

The rate of growth is also different for the two breeds. Pygmy goats tend to grow fast and uniformly. On the other hand, the Nigerian Dwarf Goats grow very slowly in their early years and then tend to pick up the pace of their growth eventually.

You see, mini goats were always raised as a dairy goat. On the other hand, pygmy goats were initially bred for their meat, although their milk quality is widely applauded today. This explains the difference in the body structure.

The next thing is the color variation. Pygmy goats are not available in as many varieties as the mini goat. The colors are black, brown and dark tan. Although the coat may have distinct markings and patterns, the base colors are very few.

In the case of the mini goats, on the other hand, they are not only available in several variations of black and brown but also in unique shades like white, cream and gold. This makes them of great interest to breeders.
The eye color also is a clear give away of the breed. While it is possible for a Nigerian Dwarf goat to have blue eyes, a pygmy goat can only have brown eyes.
With these standard qualities, you must be able to tell the difference between these two, often confusing breeds quite easily.

# Chapter 8. History of Mini Goats

Like most goat breeds that are not of native origin, the history of the Nigerian Dwarf Goats is also not very well known. The only known documents state that this breed was brought to America along with the Pygmy Goats as food to large cats that were imported, too.
In the West African region, a certain breed of goat known as the West African Mini was predominant. These goats were distributed across Africa but were concentrated in the Senegal region in the Central region and Southern Sudan.

These goats were descendants of the Central African species. The small stature of the goat was due to a type of dwarfism. The dwarfism that occurs in the goats led to shorter and plumper bodies. They also had a short head and short legs. This condition was called achondroplasia. Another type of dwarfism called pituitary hypoplasia led to smaller goats that had normal proportions.

This breed was used mostly for its meat and for the production of milk. Of course, in these regions, these goats were not really kept as pets for obvious economic reasons. Back then, these breeds were not really cultivated or grown in large numbers. They mostly thrived according to the "survival of the fittest" principal.

According to the documents of Albert Schweitzer, this breed of goat was used to provide milk for the hospital. The advantage with this breed was that it was immune to the Tse Tse fly. While most imported breeds were unable to survive this fly, this goat remained productive.

For a long time, even the Nigerian Dwarf Goats were referred to as Pygmy Goats. It was only when the breeders recognized the stark differences between the breeds that they understood that there were two unique breeds that existed. While one was stocky, the other was lean. These observations were shared globally and all the breeds agreed upon the differences. A lady named Mrs. Bonnie Abrahamson, who worked in a zoo in California, is credited with noticing the difference between the two breeds.
She coined the name Dwarves and brought several such black and white goats to the Pygmy Certification Committee. They were accepted in the herd book. However, a similar variety that was found in Indiana was rejected because it was brown in color.

That is when a petition was sent to the International Dairy Goat Registry to open a separate book for the Dwarves. In the year 1981, the first buck was included into this book with defined characteristics. In just 6 years from then, there were about 384 goats on the list.

These goats were mostly found in black, brown and gold colors. Initially, the breeders tried hard to keep these colors exclusive. However, due to the limited variations, these goats were mixed to create newer color variations. In the year 1984, the Dwarves were also accepted under the American Goat Society. The only concern that existed back then was that the genetic base of the breed was not broad enough to recognize it as a separate breed. That is why a progeny program was initiated. Soon the popularity of this breed began to grow and it still does. This was possible only after sanctioned shows that were held across the USA. Today the breed is exported to various countries across the world.

# Chapter 9. Summary of Nigerian Dwarf Goat Traits

Size: Medium Size 50 to 175 pounds or 20 to 45 kilos
Varieties Recognized: Black, Brown and Gold All the other colors and patterns are recognized.
Status: Recovering
Purpose: Domestic, Commercial and Show
Temperament: Docile and friendly
Hardiness: Can manage heat and cold. Hardy breed.
Sexual Maturity: 4 to 6 months
Breeding season: fall
No. of offspring: one or twins
These are just a few characteristics that are unique to the Nigerian Dwarf Goats. However, the breed standards have been discussed in detail in the previous chapters.

# Chapter 10. Things You Must Know About Goats as Pets

Keeping a goat at home, as exciting as it sounds, is a big deal! These are not your regular pets and are very different in terms of their needs and their behaviour.

For many people, keeping goats at home involves a very significant commercial purpose. They probably want to start a business of selling goat milk and cheese. In such cases, they have extensive knowledge about raising these animals.

On the other hand, if you want to keep pet goats at home, you need to start from scratch and gather as much information as you can about the animals and then venture into the commitment of keeping a goat.

Let us just compare a regular pet like a cat or a dog with a goat. Have you ever heard of anyone trying to milk a dog? Sounds bizarre right? However, if you do have goats at home, you need to know what to do when these animals start lactating. You see, there can be serious repercussions of not milking does when needed.

We will talk about this in greater detail. To begin with, you must really know if you want to take up the responsibility of this unique animal in the first place. There is a basic checklist that you need to go through before you bring a goat home.

I would advise every first time owner to give serious thought to the points I have mentioned below. Make sure you don't just assume that something works for you. Bringing goats home is serious business and you need to be fully convinced that you are capable of handling them.

## First Time Goat Owner's Checklist
### Can you even have a goat on your property?
Of course, this is the first thing that you need to check. You see, just having the consent of your landlord or even the fact that you have your own place, is not good enough for you to have a goat on your property. Several urban areas may be permitting people to have hens and smaller farm fowl in their backyards. However, it is a different story with goats. They are larger animals and require a special ordinance to keep them in the backyard.

If you have any doubts about this, you can speak to your local council for assistance. In case there is nothing that is officially clarified, you can still seek permission from them to legally have goats in your neighborhood. The next thing you must do is ask for permission from your neighbors. They must be ok with this. Some people may resort to complaining about you to the authorities if they are not pleased with the idea of having goats for neighbors. A few others may even try to harm your goats or just intimidate them. God forbid that you have such neighbors and the poor goat damages their property ever so slightly!

On the other hand, if you have friendly neighbors who are also keen on having goats, it is great. Then, even if your local authorities are not compliant, you can get a petition forwarded to them. If they find that your petition is valid and that you can give your goat good living conditions, they may grant you permission!

### You must get a license
Whether you are in the USA or UK, it is important to have a license and registration for your goat. You will have a local cattle association such as the American Dairy Goat Association where you can fill out a form with details such as the breed, gender and age of your goat.
Once the application is completed, you will receive an identification number that will be used to tattoo the animal as well for further reasons. So, check with your local council if you do need a license or not.

### Goats are not loners!
In most parts of my book, and in most other manuals for rearing goats, you will notice that the authors repeatedly refer to the goats in plural. This is because it is never a good idea to have a single goat in your backyard! You see goats are herd animals. They have a social structure that they need to follow in order to feel content and comfortable in the space that they are living in. In case your backyard cannot accommodate at least two goats, I suggest that you reconsider the plan of bringing home a goat.

Goats can become aggressive and may develop behavioural issues along with serious health issues if they are not in the company of other goats. Now, let us assume that you have enough space to house two goats, the next thing you need to ask yourself is whether you can afford two goats. Remember, it is twice the care, twice the attention, twice the feeding and twice the expenses if you plan to have a pair of goats in your home. So, think this through completely and speak to the other members of your family before you take that step and actually get into the demanding job of being a goat parent!

### Buying intact bucks isn't the best idea

When they are little kids, it doesn't matter whether your pet is a buck or doe. The real problems begin when your goat becomes sexually mature! This is when you really need to watch out!

You see, bucks become really aggressive when they are in heat. They can also smell very bad and can be dangerous to you and people who come to your property. This is when annoyed neighbors and even the pleasant ones will find enough reason to get your goats right out of the vicinity.
There are instances when young goats have targeted the legs of their owners. They actually ram into you and can injure you. It can be really painful even when they do not have any horns. So, you can imagine how hazardous they can be to children.

So, it is best that you bring home a spayed or neutered buck. Unless you have plans of building the herd in your farm, it is recommended that you have your buck neutered before they reach their sexual maturity. These bucks are called wethers. They are really calm and docile and are a treat to have at home.

Another thing that you need to keep in mind is that your goats need to be neutered at the right time; just before they hit puberty. They also need to be checked regularly. If they are neutered when they are too old, there is a chance that they develop urinary calculi. This is more predominant in bucks that have been neutered too early.

So, the best thing to do is just bring home a buck that has already been neutered. If you just want to have goats as pets, it is the best thing you can do. There is no need to feel guilty or unhappy about doing this. If you are not able to take your goat to the breeder at the right time for mating, you could be damaging the health of your pet. So, the wise thing to do would be to just have him neutered.

### Can you keep them confined?

There is an old saying about keeping goats and fences. It says, " If it can't hold water in, it can't hold the goat in." I tried really hard to understand what this saying meant for a long time until I began to meet with urban goat owners who presumed that a rail fence was good enough to hold the goats in.

Goats love a challenge! They will do anything to break out. They will jump over, slide under or even head butt their way out of the "strong fence" that you believe runs around your home. If you are someone who is comfortable with a 3" cyclone fence, I have news for you. Your goat can just prance over it. Yes, he doesn't even have to take a high jump!

We will talk about housing and fencing the goats in detail in the following chapters. However, I did bring it up soon to tell you that the expenses of having a goat includes preparations like putting up a newer, stronger fence. You must also be very careful with the type of fence that you choose. You want nothing that the goat can stick its head through and get stuck. If you have goat kids, you must be particularly careful, as they love to go and get stuck in the fences.

You must also know what type of fencing is really allowed in your neighbourhood. The electric fences that are usually used to keep farm animals in might be prohibited in some neighborhoods. Even a woven wire fence may require special permission in certain areas.

### *You need lots of space*
The best thing about Mini Goats is that they are extremely entertaining. They just need some space to play. You can even give them several toys outdoors to have a good time. They love to jump and climb. For young kids this is a great way to build limb coordination.

The goat is essentially an outdoor animal. More importantly, it is a rather large outdoor animal. It needs its share of exercise and fresh air.
If you live in an apartment, I hope you are considering moving out when you bring home your goats. Goats can get really miserable when they are confined to spaces inside your home. They may even get really sick, not eat that well and just be everything but themselves when they are kept locked indoors.

You see, goats are definitely getting used to the urban set up as a species. They are quite alright despite the noisy streets and the number of people that they encounter on a daily basis. But, what they really need to be in their comfort zone is the assurance of a large enough space where they can hide or run off from threats. As the owner, it is actually a wrong thing to do if you do not have enough space for your goats in your back yard.

If you really want to have a goat in your home despite the space constraints, ask yourself another question. How do you expect your goats to get any exercise if they can't run and walk around? So, there should be a large enough backyard for two goats to run around and have a good time. Then, you can definitely consider having a goat as a pet.

### *How will you take care of your goat's health?*

Goats require a lot of attention in terms of their health needs. They are more prone to parasites than most other farm animals. Goats tend to graze around when they are bored, and for food, of course. This makes them prone to several infections. It is also possible that your goat may feed on dewy grass that makes the possibility of catching an infection higher. Of course, you cannot monitor the goats all the time.

### **However, in case of an medical emergency, do you know how to deal with it?**

The biggest problem with goats is that you cannot simply take them to a regular veterinarian. There are special vets who deal with large animals like goats. So, when you do make a commitment to your goat, you also need to look for a doctor who is equipped to treat your animal.

The next thing you need to worry about is the proximity of this doctor to your home. Will you be able to take the goat to the doctor easily? More importantly, will the doctor visit your home to treat the goat when required? If you need to take your goat to the vet, you need to worry about the mode of transport you will use to take the goat to the vet.

# Conclusion

Have you ever heard of the word capricious? It basically means whimsical or rather erratic in behaviour. While goats are fun loving and calm for the most part, there are times when you cannot really predict their behavior. Also, the way your goat behaves depends largely on you. Yes, there are significant changes in the goat's behaviour when he reaches puberty or when he is well into the mating season. When it comes to the does, they are quite a handful when they are about to give birth. This is a natural cycle that you can expect from the goats.

However, if you spend enough time socializing the goats and allowing them to be around people more since they were kids, chances are that they will behave a lot better even when they are undergoing trying times biologically.

On the other hand, if your goats are left in the backyard by themselves, interacting with you only when you go up to feed them or change the water, then, you can expect a sort of distance in the way the animal deals with most people.

I have no intentions of sounding negative or discouraging. However, these are some of the real challenges that you will face when you bring home goats. If you are already having second thoughts, you may want to discuss this with your family or with other goat owners before taking the next step

.

Printed in Great Britain
by Amazon

40611838R00059